ROCKY MOUNTAIN
Gourmet Cookbook

ROCKY MOUNTAIN
Gourmet Cookbook

GOURMET RECIPES WITH
UNIQUE ROCKY MOUNTAIN APPEAL

———

LESLIE M. DEDOMINIC

FALCON®
Helena, Montana

© 1997 by Falcon® Publishing Co., Inc.

Illustrations © 1997 by Paige Moriarty

Published by Falcon® Publishing Co., Inc.
Helena and Billings, Montana

10 9 8 7 6 5 4 3 2 1

First Edition

Design, typesetting, and other prepress work by Falcon®, Helena, Montana.

Dust jacket art and all inside illustrations by Paige Moriarty.

Printed in the United States of America.

Library of Congress Cataloging in Publication Data

DeDominic, Leslie M.
    Rocky Mountain gourmet cookbook : one hundred sixty-five gourmet
recipes with unique Rocky Mountain appeal / Leslie M. DeDominic. —
1st ed.
       p.   cm.
    ISBN 1-56044-559-9
    1. Cookery, American—Western style. 2. Cookery—Rocky Mountains.
I. Title.
TX715.2.W47D44 1997   97-26441
641.5978—DC21   CIP

D e d i c a t i o n

For Tessa.

I have no hesitation about dedicating this book to you, my little Tessa. In the five years since you were born, I've felt everything from awe to terror, from frustration to the purest kind of contentment. I'd gladly relive every moment of fear in my life, just to make sure I wouldn't miss a second of the bliss I've had with you. My life, without the challenges and rewards you've brought to it, would be half-lived, kind of like a recipe without that secret ingredient. The dish may turn out okay and even be edible, but there would always be something missing.

Thank you, Tessa, for teaching me to be your mom—for helping me find that other piece of myself. No other part of my life gives me greater satisfaction than doing simple things with you, Tessa. I've especially enjoyed the culinary delights we've shared, like picking huckleberries to go in your favorite pancakes, or watching you make mud pies on the banks of the Missouri River, your occasional shouts of "keep trying, Mom" sustaining me as I cast for rainbow trout to barbecue for your dinner. Even the sweet look you get on your face when I make your favorite grilled-cheese sandwich makes me feel like the greatest chef in the West.

Now that I've got this cookbook out of the way, I'll try to stop hiding peas and carrots in something as perfect and simple as your macaroni and cheese. I love you, my Tessa Roo. Raising you to be a Montana girl, surrounded by the mountains, streams, snow, and wildlife we get to experience together, just can't be any better than heaven.

C o n t e n t s

Acknowledgments

My appreciation goes to my editors Erin Turner and Megan Hiller, and to Dana Kim for her absolutely beautiful design of this book. Rick Newby, thank you for asking me to consider publishing my cookbook.

I would like to thank all of those family and friends who have had a hand or a spoon in my development as a cooking addict and as an author.

Most especially, I'd like to thank my patient parents. Mom and Jim, thanks for your enthusiastic education of my culinary tastes on trips you took with us to expand our view of life and food. Dad, thank you for all the wild game you've shared with me over the years and for the pleasure and respect you've instilled in me for all that wild Montana has to offer.

To my sister Maureen, my brother-in-law Ron, and their children Ronni and Austin: The meals we've prepared together, while laughing, yelling children ran around the kitchen, have been a true gift to both Tessa and me.

To Aunt Fran and her daughters Amy and Ashley Mares: Thank you for your continued support during all my ups and downs and for your help with Tessa when I've needed to be working on this book.

To my grandparents: Thank you all for the rich heritage you've nurtured in me as a fifth-generation Montanan—partly through cabbage roll dinners and Butte pasties covered in gravy—and for your appreciation of the changes I often make to your traditional recipes.

Thanks to Tom Kotynski, Jackie Rice, Paula Wilmot, and Steve Shirley at the *Great Falls Tribune* for giving me the opportunity to travel around Montana for the past five years, writing about people, places, and food. I value the education and the improvement to my work your skilled editing has brought me.

To Delores Perry and Kathy Buckingham: Thank you for serving as my first cooking teachers. I hope I've learned well those lessons you taught me when I was just a teenager. And to Winfred Green Cheney, thanks for your continual culinary guidance.

Thanks to Joe DeDominic for the travels that taught me to appreciate so many different cultures and cuisines; and thanks for putting up with some of my greatest cooking fiascos.

Thanks to all my cooking buddies who have either tested or tasted my recipes or given me culinary advice, including: Debbie and Scott Anderson, Andrea and Mark Meyer, Fred and Veronica Carlton, Penny Rubner, Mary Papoulis, Joe Jewitt, Thad Suits, Jenny Smith, Kurt Tuber, Richard and Colleen Matoon, Joe and Sandy Wirth, Erin Turner and Ross Johnson, Megan Hiller and Nate Greene, Ric Bourie and Brenda Elias, Randall Green and Theresa DeLorenzo-Green, Jeff Wincapaw and Dana Kim, and most especially Eric Keszler for his fearless and exuberant consumption of every dish I've asked him to try. Eric, you've been a valued partner in culinary crime as well as a damned good fly-fishing guide.

Introduction

This cookbook is all about blending—the blending of flavors, cultures, and eras. The recipes represent a style of cooking rooted in the cuisines of early Native American tribes and of the homesteaders who came later. I have taken their incredible beginnings and dressed them up with a contemporary culinary flavor.

Various cultures that settled in the Rockies influenced these recipes, from the Pueblo Indian and Hispanic cultures in New Mexico and Colorado to the Basque sheepherders and Scottish and Irish miners in the Northern Rockies. Scarcely a culture exists that hasn't visited or settled in the Rockies, but some have a more enduring history than others.

I began cooking the Rocky Mountain gourmet way when I returned home to Montana after six years of living in other places around the country, experiencing the very different and exciting cultures I found in Texas, Mississippi, and California. When I returned to Montana, I became the chef at the Conservatory Restaurant at the Paris Gibson Square Museum of Art in Great Falls, Montana. There, I enjoyed the complete cooking luxury of being able to plan five-course menus that changed weekly with my whims. I tried to turn the job down in order to take care of my then-tiny baby, Tessa, but they convinced me to bring her along; they said I could set up a playpen in the historic music room of the old Paris Gibson High School, which had been transformed into a quaint dining room.

When visitors to this unique, contemporary art museum walked past the kitchen, they saw me in a white apron and cowboy boots with a sleeping baby in my backpack, swaying as I chopped onions and danced to radio music. At that point in my life, cooking became spiritual for me. I saw it as a way of honoring where I'd come from. I became consumed by the idea of using regional Northern Rockies ingredients, things like smoked, farm-raised pheasant from the Perry Ranch, where I'd first learned to cook, and huckleberries in tangy salad dressings. Paris Gibson Square attracted a lot of tourist traffic, and I loved hearing lunch guests wondering about this or that unusual ingredient.

I continued to explore the Rocky Mountain gourmet theme in a weekly cooking segment with Joe Lawson on KRTV in Great Falls. My friend Penny Rubner (chef at Penny's Gourmet to Go in Great Falls, Montana) and I co-hosted the show. Penny taught me how to simplify my cooking now and then, so I'd have more time to enjoy other pursuits. I'm grateful to her for the time-saving techniques, but I have to admit that I still love the day-long process of creating an elaborate meal.

These days, my favorite way to create recipes is to start with the ingredients we find most plentiful throughout the Rockies—mountain huckleberries, chokecherries, pine nuts, rosehips, wild sage, blue corn, and of course the beef, wild game, and fowl we have so close at hand.

Many recipes included in this book were inspired by fine restaurants I've visited, adapted from generous chefs, or obsessively mirrored in my own attempts to recreate tastes I've adored. Many of the recipes are followed by a cook's note, which may be an anecdote about the origin of the recipe, a personal cooking story, tips for preparing the recipe, or even an entire menu that can be built around the recipe.

I'm a very emotional cook: I tend to add more of this or less of that depending on my mood on a given day. I cook when I'm happy. I cook when I'm sad. I cook to give myself a supposedly valid excuse to pursue all my other hobbies, like fishing, hunting, berry picking, and being in the outdoors.

I'm easily converted to new forms of outdoor recreation. I garden; I cook. I hike and pick berries; I cook. I fish; I cook. I hunt; I cook. I ski; I cook. Strangely, one thing always seems to lead to the other. The night before I plan a fly-fishing trip to the Madison River, I start thinking about how wonderful a smoked pheasant salad in tangy Oriental dressing will taste as I sit at a quiet spot on the river, watching the ballet of other fly lines casting about. While standing over a flour-dusted kitchen counter, pressing chunks of beef steak into a round of pie dough to make my Grandma Dailey's Irish pasties, I can't help wishing I could head out duck hunting, so I could try this old family recipe with the wild flavor of waterfowl in place of the traditional beef in front of me.

That's how I know I was meant to be a Rocky Mountain woman. You can do so many things in one day when you live at the base of a Montana mountain just minutes from a trout-filled creek. My perfect day would look something like this: a dawn trek out to a wheat field to flush pheasant; a giddy breakfast with my little girl, Tessa, in a quiet café with country music bouncing out of the kitchen; a few hours of late autumn fly-fishing while Tessa plays with our dog Gilda on the river bank; a couple of hours spent communing with a good Richard Ford book while Tessa naps; a cozy dinner of barbecue-grilled game meat with a table of dear friends; and, maybe, a surprise snow storm that would pave the way for a midnight cross-country ski trip to the top of a mountain. Okay, maybe this is a stretch. But it could happen in the Rockies.

I guess that's what this book is all about—a way of cooking that complements a way of life. Even if you don't live in the Rockies, you can still gather a group of friends and family around a table filled with lusty, earthy, Rocky Mountain gourmet food and talk about a quiet walk in a meadow or a vacation at Glacier National Park that you still remember as if it happened just yesterday.

Filling my table until it is overflowing with food, then sharing the bounty with family and friends, is truly my most consuming passion. I hope this book gives you an appreciation for the rich cultural and culinary resources of the Rockies, from Santa Fe all the way up to Banff.

A special note about ingredients and high altitude baking:

It's best to use every food product in its freshest and purest form for the highest quality of flavor and vitamin content, but just like every other busy mom who has to use simplified or less expensive ingredients whenever she can, I make some compromises.

I'm willing to use canned green chilies instead of fresh green chilies for a quicker preparation. I also vary other ingredients according to need. My reason for sometimes listing freshly ground black pepper and sometimes listing just black pepper in an ingredient list is that it can really make a difference to have freshly ground black pepper in a salad dressing or a pasta dish with lots of fresh ingredients. When freshly ground pepper is less likely to create a distinct taste, I list just plain black pepper in a recipe and let the cook make the choice. The same goes for the recipes where I've listed olive oil and not extra virgin olive oil. I prefer the rich, fresh olive flavor of extra virgin olive oil and find it irreplaceable in certain recipes. Extra virgin olive oil is more expensive, though, so when it isn't truly necessary to the flavor combination of a recipe I list just olive oil and leave it up to the cook and the cook's pocketbook to decide.

High altitude can be a consideration for Rocky Mountain cooks. Baking, in particular, may require adjustments to ingredients, temperature, and baking times. The recipes in this book are based on normal sea level requirements. However, for those bakers at particularly high altitudes, you'll want to do some experimenting to see what works at a specific altitude. Reducing the amount of leavening (baking powder) in a cake or quick-bread recipe is usually effective in preventing the sunken-cake effect. Adding 2 tablespoons of extra water and reducing the sugar by a tablespoon or two is also helpful. To prevent yeast breads from falling, punch the dough down twice. You may also need less flour to achieve the right dough consistency. While baking at high altitudes, lower oven temperatures by 10–20°.

 Low Fat Where recipes in this book are designated lowfat, 30 percent or less of the calories are from fat.

APPETIZERS

Red Chili Onion Rings

Parmesan Spinach Balls with Green Chili- Honey-Mustard Sauce

Trout Cakes with Rosehip Citrus Mayonnaise

Leslie's Black Bean Salsa

Black Bean and Jalapeño Quesadillas

Hot Oyster Sauté

Easy Sun-dried Tomato Foccacia with Feta

Spicy Buffalo-Stuffed Mushrooms

Creamy Cilantro Hummus

Dried Mushroom Caviar

Huckleberry Brie En Croute

Chili-Pickled Chicken Wings

RED CHILI ONION RINGS

3–4 cups vegetable oil for frying

2$\frac{1}{2}$ tablespoons hot chili powder

$\frac{1}{2}$ teaspoon cayenne pepper

$\frac{1}{2}$ teaspoon cumin

$\frac{1}{2}$ teaspoon salt

$\frac{1}{4}$ teaspoon black pepper

1$\frac{1}{2}$ cups flour

4 large yellow onions, peeled and sliced into thin rings

Using an electric deep-fat fryer or a deep pan on the stove top, heat at least 2 inches of oil in the bottom of pan to 325° on a thermometer.

Combine the seasonings and flour in a plastic zip-closure-style bag.

Separate the sliced onions into individual rings, so they don't clump together. Drop a handful of onions into the flour bag and shake well.

Add the flour-coated onion rings to the hot oil and fry, stirring several times, for about 3–5 minutes, until the onions are golden brown. Remove the onion rings with a slotted spoon and drain on paper towels.

Serve warm as an appetizer or as a side dish with steaks or grilled fish.

Serves 8–10.

The chili seasoning in this breading is terrific on a variety of vegetables, so play around with it. Use mushrooms, broccoli, carrot spears, cauliflower, yam slices, and even whole cloves of garlic. I also enjoy adding $\frac{1}{2}$ cup of cornmeal to this breading for a nuttier, sweeter-tasting, differently textured variation. If you add the cornmeal, you can also drop a few peeled shrimp into the bag for a slight twist on Cajun popcorn shrimp.

PARMESAN SPINACH BALLS WITH GREEN CHILI- HONEY-MUSTARD SAUCE

Sauce:
- 1 4-ounce can diced green chilies
- ½ cup Dijon mustard
- ¼ cup honey
- ⅛ teaspoon cayenne pepper

Balls:
- 3 cups crushed seasoned dry bread stuffing
- 2 10-ounce packages frozen chopped spinach, thawed and drained
- ½ cup butter, melted
- ¼ cup finely minced red onion

- 1 clove garlic, crushed
- ½ teaspoon thyme
- 1 tablespoon Louisiana-style red pepper sauce
- 1 teaspoon soy sauce
- 1½ cups grated Parmesan cheese
- 3 eggs, slightly beaten
- ½ teaspoon salt
- ¼ teaspoon black pepper

Heat the sauce ingredients in a small saucepan over medium heat (or use a microwave to heat the sauce), stirring well.

Preheat oven to 375°.

In a large mixing bowl, combine all the ingredients for the spinach balls, stirring well. Let the mixture sit for 10 minutes so the liquids have a chance to soften the bread crumbs.

Stir the mixture again. Form it into balls about 1½ inches in diameter. Place the balls on a baking sheet and bake for 15 minutes. Use a spatula to turn the spinach balls over. Bake for another 10 minutes or until firm and crisp on the outside.

Serve with the warm Green Chili- Honey-Mustard Sauce.

Makes about 40 balls.

This is my own version of my friend Debbie Anderson's easy make-ahead recipe. She frequently freezes batches in plastic bags and reheats them in the oven or over a campfire.

While each course of a backcountry meal doesn't have to be a gourmet selection, it enhances the trip if you've taken the time to prepare something ahead, be it an appetizer, entrée, or dessert, that's a bit out of the ordinary. Choose items that are firm enough to withstand being tucked into a backpack, are light in weight, and fit well into resealable plastic bags. Then use them to highlight a meal of the more typical dried grains and pastas that tend to be backcountry-friendly.

TROUT CAKES WITH ROSEHIP CITRUS MAYONNAISE

Rosehip Citrus Mayonnaise:

 2 tablespoons orange juice concentrate

 ¹/₄ cup rosehip powder

 ¹/₂ cup white wine

 1 tablespoon Louisiana-style hot sauce

 ¹/₄ cup country-style mustard

 1 cup mayonnaise

Trout Cakes:

 2 pounds boneless and skinless trout fillets, baked, cooled, and separated into flakes

 ¹/₄ cup minced red onion

 ¹/₄ cup minced celery

 ¹/₄ cup minced red bell pepper

 1 clove garlic, crushed

 1 tablespoon orange juice concentrate

 2 tablespoons lemon juice

 1 teaspoon Louisiana-style hot sauce

 2 eggs, slightly beaten

 ¹/₂ cup fine dry bread crumbs

 ¹/₂ teaspoon thyme

 salt and pepper to taste

 ¹/₂ cup cornmeal

 non-stick cooking spray

To make the sauce, combine the orange juice concentrate, rosehip powder, white wine, and hot sauce in a small saucepan over medium heat. Whisk until bubbly and smooth. Remove from heat and let cool for 10 minutes.

Whisk the mustard and mayonnaise into the rosehip mixture. Refrigerate until cool.

In a large mixing bowl, use your hands to gently combine all the ingredients for the trout cakes except the cornmeal. Mix until everything is well incorporated. Pat the mixture into 8 patties, each about an inch thick. Cover well and refrigerate for at least 2 hours but not more than 12 hours.

Spray a skillet with non-stick spray and heat it to medium-high temperature.

Place the cornmeal on a plate and rub both sides of each trout cake in the cornmeal. Brown the trout cakes in the skillet for about 5 minutes on each side. Serve warm with a dollop of Rosehip Citrus Mayonnaise on each cake.

Makes 8 trout cakes.

I try to cook with smaller trout, less than 12 inches long. The larger pockets of fat in older trout tend to carry a muddier taste. Also pay attention to the eyes, to be sure they haven't been sitting in the display case too long. Fresh trout have shiny eyes; not-so-fresh trout have cloudy eyes. Finally, if trout, farm-raised or stream-caught, smells strange or very strong, it's doubtful the cooked flesh will taste good. Make sure the fish has a freshwater scent that is not pungent in any way.

LESLIE'S BLACK BEAN SALSA

2 cups cooked black beans, canned or homemade, drained

1 cup diced scallions

1 green bell pepper, diced

1 red bell pepper, diced

3 cloves garlic, crushed

3 cups coarsely diced fresh ripe tomatoes

4 tablespoons balsamic vinegar

2 teaspoons hot chili powder

1 teaspoon cumin

1 teaspoon oregano

½ teaspoon cayenne pepper, (or to taste)

1 teaspoon sugar

1 teaspoon salt

¼ teaspoon black pepper

2 15-ounce cans Mexican-style stewed tomatoes

1 15-ounce can tomato sauce

½ cup minced cilantro leaves

1 7-ounce can green chilies, diced

Stir all the ingredients together in a large sealable container. Refrigerate for at least 2 hours before serving to allow the flavors to combine.

Serve this hearty salsa over burritos, with eggs, or with tortilla chips.

Makes about 8 cups.

I first tried black bean salsa before salsa became the world's most highly consumed condiment. My friend Penny Rubner made it in the kitchen of her deli, Penny's Gourmet to Go in Great Falls, Montana, while we were taping a segment of our KRTV cooking program together. Now, Penny would tell me for sure that I've added too many ingredients to a simple fresh salsa, and she might be right. Always trying to make her recipes fun and as little work as possible, Penny is great at the art of simplification.

BLACK BEAN AND JALAPEÑO QUESADILLAS

2½ cups grated jalapeño pepper cheese

¼ cup minced cilantro leaves

1–2 fresh jalapeño peppers, finely minced

5 scallions, diced

½ teaspoon cumin

½ cup diced red bell pepper

10 large flour tortillas

1¼ cups cooked black beans, canned or
     homemade, drained

non-stick cooking spray

In a mixing bowl, combine the grated cheese, cilantro, jalapeños, scallions, cumin, and red peppers. Toss, mixing the ingredients well.

Heat a skillet over medium-high heat and spray it with non-stick cooking spray.

Lay one tortilla in the skillet. Spread ½ cup of the cheese mixture over the tortilla. Scatter ¼ cup black beans over the cheese and sprinkle another couple of tablespoons of cheese over the beans. Cover with another tortilla. Brown for 3–5 minutes, until the cheese melts, and carefully flip the quesadilla over. Brown the second side for 3 minutes.

Remove the quesadilla to a waiting plate and repeat with the remaining tortillas and ingredients. Slice the quesadillas into wedges and serve with salsa and guacamole.

Makes 5 quesadillas.

Tortillas are another one of those foods that have made their way into the mainstream of the American diet, and I wonder how I ever got along without them. An easy-to-transport form of bread, tortillas don't get smashed in the grocery sack or take up a bunch of space in the refrigerator. On ranches like the Gray Ranch in Animas, New Mexico, or the Hurt Ranch in Hachita, New Mexico, the tortilla is used as a handy package, holding basics like steak, potatoes, or beans for crews of cowboys who want something hearty to hold off the growling in their stomachs until mealtime. Quesadillas can be filled with any combination of your favorite ingredients. See page 157 for a Whole Wheat-Red Pepper Tortilla recipe.

HOT OYSTER SAUTÉ

 4 tablespoons butter
$1/3$ cup finely minced red onion
$1/3$ cup finely minced celery
 2 10-ounce jars of oysters
$1/4$ cup merlot or cabernet wine
 2 cloves garlic, crushed
$1/2$ teaspoon thyme
$1/2$ teaspoon rosemary
$1/2$ teaspoon parsley
$1/8$ teaspoon sage
$1/8$ teaspoon red pepper flakes
$1/2$ teaspoon salt

$1/4$ teaspoon black pepper
 1 teaspoon teriyaki sauce
 1 tablespoon dry sherry
 1 cup fine dry bread crumbs
$1/2$ cup freshly grated Parmesan cheese
$1/2$ cup grated Swiss cheese

thin slices of sourdough baguette,
    lightly toasted

Preheat the oven to 375°.

Melt the butter in a skillet over medium heat. Sauté the onions and celery in the butter until soft, about 8 minutes. Add the oysters, wine, garlic, herbs, salt, black pepper, teriyaki, and sherry. Stir and sauté for 3 more minutes. Pour the oyster mixture into an oven-safe ceramic serving dish.

In a bowl, combine the bread crumbs and cheeses. Mix well, then sprinkle over the oysters. Bake for about 10 minutes, or until just heated through.

Serve with sourdough baguette slices. Makes about 4 cups oyster spread, enough for 6–8 people as an appetizer.

If you saw this recipe with oysters in it and wondered if I might be trying to sneak in some of those strange Rocky Mountain oysters you've heard about—the ones served after branding time at ranches or in little bars in out-of-the-way places like Dubois, Wyoming, or Square Butte, Montana—don't worry. The real sea-faring shellfish type of oyster has been part of Rocky Mountain cooking since the 1800s, when jars of them arrived in grocery stores for traditional holiday feasts.

As for the Rocky Mountain variety—yes, we have been known to eat the testicles of calves at festivals and as a quirky snack in bars and homes up and down this region. For the uninitiated: Rocky Mountain oysters remind me of gizzards, with a rich chewy meat similar to many organ delicacies. There aren't a whole lot of ways to eat calf testicles. They are usually sliced into quarter-inch horizontal pieces, breaded, and fried.

EASY SUN-DRIED TOMATO FOCCACIA WITH FETA

2 tablespoons cornmeal

1 loaf frozen bread dough, thawed and set to rise in a warm place for 1 hour

2 cloves garlic, crushed

$1/4$ teaspoon freshly ground black pepper

$1/4$ teaspoon salt

$1/2$ teaspoon rosemary

3 tablespoons extra virgin olive oil

$1/2$ cup diced sun-dried tomatoes, plumped in hot water for 15 minutes, then drained

$3/4$ cup crumbled feta cheese

good-quality extra virgin olive oil for dipping

Preheat the oven to 375°. Dust a baking or pizza pan with the cornmeal, spreading it over the entire pan.

Use a rolling pin to roll the dough into a 1-inch-thick round, pulling it into shape with your fingertips. Place the dough on the baking pan and poke your finger into the surface to make a bumpy texture.

Whisk the garlic, pepper, salt, rosemary, olive oil, and tomatoes together in a small bowl, combining well. Use a spoon to ladle this mixture onto the bread dough, spreading it all over the round and distributing the tomatoes.

Bake the foccacia for 10 minutes. Sprinkle the feta cheese on top and bake for another 5–10 minutes, until golden.

Serve in wedges with a dish of olive oil in the center of the table for dipping.

Serves 6–8.

This is another one of those gourmet knock-offs I feel compelled to provide for those cooks who don't have time to do every course of a meal from scratch. Now that I've confessed to not being a pure gourmet all the time, I'd encourage some playing around with frozen-bread-dough foccacia. Some other toppings to mix into the garlic olive oil include: grated fresh lemon rind, walnuts, and blue cheese; slices of dried apples, almonds, and cheddar; a melange of different kinds of olives, from green to black to bitter Greek—all coarsely chopped; diced green chilies, thin rings of red onion, and pine nuts; smoked oysters, strips of red bell pepper, and lumps of goat cheese; and the Cilantro Pesto from (page 74), grated fresh ginger, diced scallions, and sliced shitake mushrooms. Also, you can try any of these combinations with the homemade foccacia recipe (page 159).

Low Fat

SPICY BUFFALO-STUFFED MUSHROOMS

1 pound firm white mushrooms
   with the stems removed

½ pound lean buffalo, elk, or beef burger

2 cloves garlic, crushed

½ teaspoon red pepper flakes

½ teaspoon salt

¼ teaspoon black pepper

2 tablespoons Worcestershire sauce

4 tablespoons hot mustard

½ teaspoon oregano

¼ teaspoon sage

½ cup fine dry bread crumbs

1 egg, slightly beaten

1 cup beef broth

½ teaspoon Tabasco pepper sauce

Clean the mushrooms with a paper towel or mushroom brush.

Preheat the oven to 375°.

In a mixing bowl, combine the remaining ingredients, except the broth and pepper sauce, stirring well. Fill the mushrooms with the meat mixture, packing them tightly until the filling forms a small mound above the mushroom.

Pour the beef broth and pepper sauce into the bottom of a 9 x 13-inch cake pan. Arrange the mushrooms in the broth. Bake for 20 minutes, testing to make sure the meat is cooked before removing from the heat.

Serve hot in a chafing dish.

Makes 10–15 mushrooms.

Buffalo meat is a popular Rocky Mountain ingredient, but you are unlikely to find it in any grocery-store meat department. See Appendix A for sources for this delicious, lean meat.

CREAMY CILANTRO HUMMUS

1 cup dried chick peas, soaked in water
   overnight and drained

$^1/_2$ teaspoon salt

3 cloves garlic, crushed

4 tablespoons fresh lemon juice

3 tablespoons extra virgin olive oil

$^1/_2$ teaspoon cumin

$^3/_4$ cup sour cream

$^1/_4$ cup fresh cilantro leaves

pita bread, sliced pie-fashion into triangles
   and toasted

In a medium-sized saucepan, cover the chick peas in water. Add the salt and 1 clove of crushed garlic. Bring to a boil, then reduce the heat and simmer until the peas are tender, about 50 minutes. Drain and cool.

Place the cooked, cooled chick peas, remaining 2 cloves of garlic, lemon juice, olive oil, and cumin in a food processor and blend until smooth. Add the sour cream and cilantro and blend again until all the ingredients are incorporated. You may need to add salt and pepper to taste.

Serve with toasted pita bread triangles.

Makes 3 cups.

I usually serve this hummus on wedges of toasted pita bread, an eastern flat bread that makes a hollow pocket when baked. Pita bread is one of those bakery shelf items that provides a variety of snacking possibilities with very little cooking effort. The rounds are usually sliced into two half-moons, separated to create a pocket, and stuffed with savory fillings. I like to expand their use—they make perfect appetizer scoops.

Slice each round like you would a pie, into about 8 wedges. Then separate the top and bottom of each wedge, ripping at the rounded edge to create two pieces. Brush each piece with olive oil or melted butter to which you've added any number of flavorings—crushed garlic, puréed jalapeño pepper, or $^1/_2$ teaspoon or less of spices or herbs like curry, thyme, cumin, cinnamon, salt, pepper, or any combination that sounds fun. For a package of 8 pita breads, $^1/_3$ cup of oil or melted butter will be plenty. Lay the seasoned pitas on a baking sheet and toast in a 400° oven until just golden, about 8–12 minutes.

DRIED MUSHROOM CAVIAR

2 pounds mushrooms, coarsely chopped—use white or combine a variety of mushrooms for unique flavors

3 tablespoons olive oil

1/4 cup diced red onion

1/4 cup diced red bell pepper

2 cloves garlic, crushed

1/2 teaspoon salt

1/4 teaspoon freshly ground black pepper

2 tablespoons balsamic vinegar

2 teaspoons fermented Oriental fish sauce

1/2 teaspoon thyme

baguette slices

Preheat the oven to 300°.

Spread the chopped mushrooms on a baking sheet and bake for 1 hour, stirring several times. Set the mushrooms aside.

Heat the olive oil in a skillet over medium heat. Sauté the onion, bell pepper, and garlic in the oil for 8 minutes. Add the mushrooms and the remaining ingredients (except the bread) to the vegetables in the skillet and toss to incorporate the flavors evenly. Refrigerate the caviar overnight.

Let the caviar come to room temperature before serving. Spoon it into a crock and serve with baguette slices to spread it on.

Makes 2 1/2 cups.

I like this caviar with Merlot or Cabernet Sauvignon.

HUCKLEBERRY BRIE EN CROUTE

1 medium-sized wheel of Brie,
  about 6 inches in diameter
8 sheets frozen phyllo pastry
3 tablespoons melted butter
½ cup huckleberry jam
apple wedges
water crackers

Preheat the oven to 375°. Grease a baking sheet. Thaw frozen phyllo dough, making sure to keep covered and chilled.

Lay 1 sheet of phyllo on the countertop, brush it with butter, and cover it with another phyllo sheet. Repeat until all 8 sheets of phyllo have been used.

Spread the huckleberry jam on top of the brie wheel. Place the layers of phyllo dough on top of the brie, centering the wheel under the phyllo. Make sure to lift the phyllo sheets carefully; you may need to use a couple of spatulas to help move the phyllo on top of the brie.

Tuck the edges of the phyllo under the the brie, overlapping them. Place the Brie seam side down on the greased baking sheet and bake for about 20 minutes, until golden and soft.

Remove the brie wheel from the oven and transfer it to a serving plate. Serve it with sliced apples and water crackers.

Serves 8–10.

Sometimes I want to entertain friends, but a sit-down meal doesn't fit into our plans for the evening. My second favorite way to feed people is with an appetizer buffet. A buffet allows you to fill people with a hearty variety of foods quickly and with a certain flair. I try to make sure to balance my appetizer selections so they include veggies, fruits, cheeses, meats, and breads, with a choice among sweet, salty, sour, and spicy finger foods.

Suggested Appetizer Buffet Menu:
- Creamy Cilantro Hummus with pita bread (page 14)
- Spicy Buffalo-Stuffed Mushrooms (page 13)
- Chili-Pickled Chicken Wings (page 17)
- Huckleberry Brie En Croute
- Flathead Cherry Fudge Torte (page 130)

CHILI-PICKLED CHICKEN WINGS

2 pounds chicken wings, cleaned and rinsed

1 teaspoon salt

1 tablespoon Tabasco pepper sauce

1/4 teaspoon red pepper flakes

1/4 teaspoon black pepper

3 cloves garlic, crushed

1/2 cup finely minced red onion

1 teaspoon oregano

2 cups cider vinegar

Combine all the ingredients in a large sealed container. Shake well. Refrigerate the mixture for three days, shaking the container at least twice a day.

Preheat the oven to 375°.

Pour the contents of the sealed container into a large casserole dish with a lid. Cover the dish and bake for 40 minutes. Remove the dish from the oven. Using tongs, lift the chicken wings out of the vinegar marinade to a waiting baking sheet.

Increase the oven temperature to 400°. Return the chicken wings to bake until browned, about 15 minutes. Serve warm or cold.

Makes 25–30 wings.

The idea for Chili-Pickled Chicken Wings came to me when a group of friends and I were talking about German food—specifically, the roast called sauerbraten, which is essentially pickled. I'm partial to vinegar flavors in my cooking. I crave sweet and sour combinations, as well as hot and sour ones. Sour flavors seem to wake up the tongue, making way for other tastes.

When I'm planning a meal, I keep in mind something a foods class professor told me at The University of Montana in Missoula. She said we'd overeat less often if we took greater care in our meal planning to satisfy all areas of our tongue. Different flavors are perceived by separate areas of the tongue's surface. She said that if we had a little bit of sour, a little bit of sweet, a little bit of spicy hot, and a little bit of salty flavor, our tongues would quickly tell our brains that we were satisfied. I'm not sure where my professor came up with this theory, but it rings true for me.

SOUPS AND STEWS

Zuni Posole Stew with Pork

African Peanut–Carrot Soup

Potato, Cheese, and Chili Bisque

Southwestern Butternut Squash Soup

Rocky Mountain Cioppino

Hot and Sour Soup with Mountain Fish Won Tons

Fresh Vegetable Soup

Green Chili Stew

Native Bullet Soup

White Minestrone

Scandinavian Berry Fruit Soup with Cinnamon

Bacon–Lentil Soup Au Vin

Beer Bread Soup with Cabbage

Trapper's Beef Jerky Soup

Chicken and White Bean Chili with Shoepeg Corn

Elk and Black Bean Chili

Curried Almond Rice Soup

Zucchini–Buttermilk Soup

Trout in Lemon Broth with Peas

ZUNI POSOLE STEW WITH PORK

1 tablespoon vegetable oil

1 pound pork shoulder, trimmed of fat and cut into 1-inch cubes

1 medium-sized onion, diced

1 green bell pepper, seeded and diced

2 cloves garlic, crushed

3 cups dried posole (corn)

1 7-ounce can green chilies or 4 fresh Anaheim chilies, diced

1½ teaspoons ground cumin

1 tablespoon oregano

¼ teaspoon cinnamon

1 teaspoon red pepper flakes (or to taste)

2 teaspoons salt

¼ teaspoon black pepper

3 quarts water

In a large stock pot over medium-high heat, sauté the pork in the oil until brown.

Add the onion, bell pepper, and garlic and sauté an additional 5 minutes, stirring frequently.

Add the remaining ingredients, using enough water at one time to keep the posole covered. Bring to a boil and reduce the heat to low. Cover the pot and simmer for 4–5 hours or until the posole corn is tender. You may need to add more salt and red pepper flakes before serving, according to your taste.

Serves 10.

Posole is a traditional New Mexican stew that the Pueblo Indians serve on feast days. As you can see, it doesn't require a lot of attention; it's a great meal to leave on the stove while you have a house full of company.

Nowadays you can often find posole—the corn—in the ethnic section of many markets. Some grocery managers who don't stock it have been happy to order it for me. Posole is usually a white field corn, like hominy, that is washed in lime to remove the outer husk of each kernel. I also like the blue corn posole that I've found lately.

This stew is hearty even without the pork, if you want to use it as a side dish or as a vegetarian meal. For my vegetarian friends, I add black beans to make a complete protein dish.

AFRICAN PEANUT-CARROT SOUP

2 tablespoons butter

1 medium onion, finely diced

2 stalks celery, finely diced

2 cloves garlic, crushed

2 tablespoons all-purpose flour

4 cups chicken broth

2 teaspoons cumin

1 tablespoon grated fresh ginger root

1/2 teaspoon ground coriander

3/4 teaspoon salt

1/4 teaspoon black pepper

1/4–1/2 teaspoon cayenne pepper

2 cups cooked, puréed carrots, fresh or canned (use a food processor or blender)

1/2 cup chunky peanut butter

1/2 cup half-and-half

fresh cilantro leaves for garnish

Melt the butter in a large stock pot over medium heat. Sauté the onion, celery, and garlic in the butter until soft.

Add the flour to this mixture and stir for about 2 minutes to dissolve. Whisk the chicken broth into the pot, taking care to keep the mixture smooth.

Add the remaining ingredients except the cilantro. Stir and let simmer for 15–20 minutes, until thickened and aromatic.

Serve garnished with fresh cilantro leaves. Serves 6.

During a visit to the Grand Tetons, those forever white peaks that loom over Jackson Hole, Wyoming, I met a kindly gentleman named Loring Woodman at a gas station. He described himself as the owner of the Darwin Ranch, a dude ranch that specialized in fly fishing and pack trips around the Jackson Hole area. He suggested I head one block off the town square, with its distinctive antler arch, for a meal at the Sweetwater Inn.

At the Sweetwater I enjoyed a comforting yet exciting bowl of soup—a cream-based peanut-carrot soup. As soon as I arrived back home in Great Falls, I set out to recreate this exotic, creamy soup and have long been pleased with the results.

POTATO, CHEESE, AND CHILI BISQUE

¼ cup butter or margarine

1 medium onion, chopped

1 clove garlic, crushed

¼ cup all-purpose flour

6 cups chicken broth—canned or homemade

6 medium potatoes, peeled and sliced into ½-inch cubes

1½ teaspoons ground cumin

1 teaspoon salt

¼ teaspoon freshly ground black pepper

2 cups whole milk

2 cups grated medium cheddar cheese

1 7-ounce can diced green chilies

2–3 dashes hot pepper sauce (or to taste)

In a soup pot, sauté the onions and garlic in the butter until soft over medium-high heat. Add the flour and stir for 2 minutes to dissolve.

Add the broth, potatoes, cumin, salt, and pepper. Cover the soup pot and simmer over medium-low heat for 25–30 minutes, until potatoes are falling apart.

Add the milk, cheese, chilies, and hot sauce. Heat for a few more minutes and serve.

Serves 6.

Everything about New Mexican cooking delights my culinary curiosity, especially the chilies. Chilies take center stage during the Grants, New Mexico, Chili Fiesta held annually in September. Whether you make it to a fiesta or not, it's not hard to find fresh-roasted chilies in New Mexico and even up into Colorado during the autumn months. I can still remember the scent of fresh green chilies being loaded into a giant turning roaster over a fire every Saturday morning at the Santa Fe farmers market. You can buy a whole garbage bag full of them, and then spend the rest of the day peeling them, your eyes and throat burning. But when you taste that first bite of chili relleno, it seems worth the effort.

Chili is the most important flavor in this soup, so it is best if you can get fresh chilies and roast them yourself.

SOUTHWESTERN BUTTERNUT SQUASH SOUP

1 cup chopped onion

³/₄ cup chopped leeks, white sections only

2¹/₂ cups peeled and diced raw butternut squash—or use pumpkin or acorn squash

¹/₄ cup sherry

¹/₄ teaspoon freshly grated or ground nutmeg

¹/₄ teaspoon ground cumin

pinch of cinnamon

¹/₈ teaspoon grated fresh ginger root

³/₄ teaspoon salt

¹/₄ teaspoon freshly ground black pepper

¹/₈ teaspoon cayenne pepper, or to taste

4 cups chicken or vegetable stock

non-stick cooking spray

Spray the bottom of a stock pot with cooking spray. Sauté the onions and leeks over medium heat until they wilt. If they begin to brown, add 3 tablespoons of water or chicken broth to the pan.

Once the onions and leeks begin to soften, add the remaining ingredients to the pot and bring to a boil. Cover the pot, reduce the heat, and simmer for about 20 minutes, until the squash begins to fall apart.

Remove the pot from the heat. In a food processor or blender, purée the mixture in 3 or 4 batches until very smooth. Return the soup to the pot to reheat before serving, or let the soup cool and refrigerate it for up to 5 days.

Serves 4–6.

This is a very lowfat, flavorful, and vitamin-packed soup for a chilly day, but it can also be served to guests in various elegant ways. It can be dressed up (with a little imagination) or used as a sauce for pasta. Consider this serving option:

Split several more butternut squash in half (depending on the number of guests). Hollow out their centers and bake them in a 350° oven for 30–40 minutes or until tender. Ladle the prepared, heated soup into the hollow of each squash. Serve with a dollop of Chantilly cream and a dusting of grated nutmeg on top. To make Chantilly cream, combine equal parts whipped cream and sour cream.

**Low
Fat**

ROCKY MOUNTAIN CIOPPINO

2 teaspoons extra virgin olive oil

1 large onion, coarsely chopped

2 cloves garlic, crushed

1 red bell pepper, seeded and sliced into
 short strips

3 carrots, peeled and sliced in 2-inch lengths

3 cups baby red potatoes or regular
 red potatoes cut into 1-inch cubes

1 tablespoon minced chipotle chilies

3 cups clam juice

2 cups red wine—Zinfandel or Merlot are best

1 28-ounce can diced stewed tomatoes,
 juice included

1 cup tomato sauce

1 7-ounce can diced green chilies—
 mild or hot depending on desired taste

1 teaspoon oregano

1 teaspoon thyme

1 teaspoon rosemary

¼ cup minced fresh cilantro

18 bay scallops

1½ pounds medium-sized shrimp,
 peeled and deveined

12 clams, well-scrubbed

12 mussels, well-scrubbed

1 pound sea bass, pike, or other firm fish,
 cut into 2-inch cubes

Heat the olive oil in a large stock pot over medium heat. Sauté the onion, garlic, and pepper until soft.

Add the remaining ingredients except the cilantro and seafood. Stir and simmer, covered, for about 20 minutes or until the vegetables are soft. At this stage, the stew can be removed from the heat, stored in the refrigerator for up to 2 days, and reheated.

Add the cilantro and seafood, cover the pot, and steam until the clams open, about 3–5 minutes.

Serve immediately with crushed red pepper flakes sprinkled over the top, if desired.

Serves 6.

This is an adulterated version of a classic San Francisco-style stew created by Portuguese fishermen. I've introduced Rocky Mountain ingredients to it to add fire and unique flavors. Serve Rocky Mountain Cioppino with a big green salad topped with Balsamic Vinaigrette (page 49); a creamy soft cheese; lots of Red Zinfandel or Merlot wine; a crusty, dense Italian-style bread; and the Chocolate Mocha Biscotti (page 126) for a lively meal with friends.

Low
Fat

HOT AND SOUR SOUP WITH MOUNTAIN FISH WON TONS

1 tablespoon hot chili-sesame oil

24 2-inch cubes firm fish—try pike or bass

1/4 cup finely diced onion

1/4 cup finely diced red bell pepper

2 cloves garlic, crushed and divided

24 store-bought won ton wrappers

2 tablespoons grated fresh ginger root

6 cups chicken broth

1/4 cup grated carrot

1/4 cup diced scallions

6 tablespoons freshly squeezed lemon juice

1 tablespoon soy sauce

1/2 teaspoon red pepper sauce like Tabasco (or to taste)

diced scallions and red pepper flakes for garnish

Heat the sesame oil in a sauté pan over medium heat. Add the the fish, onion, red pepper, and one clove of the garlic and sauté for 3 minutes. Remove from the heat.

Lay out the won ton wrappers. Place 1 piece of fish and a teaspoonful of the sautéed vegetables in the center of each won ton. Dip a finger in water and run it around the edges of the won ton wrapper, then fold it in half to create a triangle. Press the edges to seal. Pinch two ends of the triangle together to form a little ring at one end of the won ton. Repeat with the other won tons. Set aside.

Mix the remaining ingredients (except the garnish) together in a stock pot. Heat over medium-high heat. Once the soup has come to a boil, add the won tons carefully so they don't fall apart. Boil for 3–5 minutes, until the wrappers are translucent.

Serve immediately, 4 won tons per bowl, with a sprinkle of diced scallions and red pepper flakes on top.

Serves 6.

In just about any little town up and down the Rockies, the spirit of the West includes a rich diversity of cultures. "Western cooking" often calls up an image of a barbecued steak or a pot of beans. But the phrase reminds me of a pungent, tangy, spicy soup I had at a terrific little restaurant in Ketchum, Idaho, called the China Pepper. The menu at this innovative restaurant blends Thai, Hunan, and Szechwan cuisines in a way that pays true homage to several different groups of western pioneers. My Hot and Sour Soup with Mountain Fish Won Tons is inspired by the China Pepper menu.

Low Fat

FRESH VEGETABLE SOUP

1 tablespoon vegetable oil

1 large onion, diced

1 clove garlic, crushed

1 cup navy beans, soaked in water for at least 4 hours

2 quarts chicken or vegetable stock

2 cups chopped cabbage

3 large carrots, cubed

4 medium unpeeled potatoes, cubed

1 cup cut string beans

1 cup fresh or frozen corn

1 14-ounce can diced stewed tomatoes, juice included

2 bay leaves

1/4 teaspoon celery seed

1/8 cup minced fresh parsley

1/2 cup minced fresh dill

1 1/2 teaspoons salt

1/4 teaspoon black pepper

juice of 1 lemon

sour cream and fresh dill for garnish

In a large stock pot over medium heat, sauté the onion and garlic in the oil until soft. Add the navy beans and stock and bring to a boil. Cover, reduce the heat, and simmer for 40 minutes.

Add the remaining ingredients except the lemon juice and garnish. Stir and bring to a boil again. Reduce the heat and simmer, uncovered, for about 20–30 minutes until the vegetables are tender.

Add the lemon juice and adjust the salt and pepper seasoning to taste. Serve in bowls with a dollop of sour cream and fresh dill for garnish.

Serves 8–10.

Great Falls, Montana, where I grew up, is located near several Hutterite colonies. I used to see Hutterites around town in their distinctive clothing—black pants, suspenders, and beards on the men; polka-dot kerchiefs, uniquely rolled hair, and colorful long skirts on the women.

A sect of the Anabaptist groups that came from Moravia, the Hutterites settled in Montana and Canada. Much like the Mennonites and Amish who settled in other parts of the country, the Hutterites believe in communal living, pacifism, and simplicity. They are excellent farmers, and in contrast to the Amish, they use modern equipment. Their rich culture is evident in sturdy handmade baskets, lilting songs from the old country, and food that is mostly German and eastern European in origin.

This recipe for a light but hearty vegetable soup is similar to one of many *suppen* served for supper in Hutterite colonies around Montana one night a week during the winter. The Hutterites add pork sausage for extra energy.

Low
Fat

GREEN CHILI STEW

1 pound pork tenderloin, trimmed of fat and cut into 1-inch cubes

1 large onion, diced

3 cloves garlic, crushed

2 tablespoons vegetable oil

2 tablespoons flour

2 cups fresh, roasted, peeled, seeded, and chopped New Mexican green chilies

2 teaspoons oregano

2 teaspoons ground cumin

1/2 teaspoon red pepper flakes

3 large potatoes, peeled and cubed

1 14-ounce can stewed tomatoes, diced, juice included

1 green bell pepper, seeded and diced

2 carrots, peeled and cubed

4 cups chicken broth

1/2 teaspoon salt

1/4 teaspoon black pepper

1/2 cup white wine

1/4 cup minced fresh cilantro leaves

pine nuts and red pepper flakes for garnish

In a large stock pot over medium-high heat, sauté the pork, onions, and garlic in the oil until soft. Add the flour and stir until dissolved, about 3–5 minutes.

Add the remaining ingredients except the cilantro and garnish. Stir well and bring to a boil. Reduce the heat and simmer, uncovered, for about 30 minutes or until the potatoes are tender. Remove from heat.

Stir in the cilantro and serve, garnished with pine nuts and red pepper flakes. This stew keeps well in refrigerator for up to 4 days, and tastes even better the second day.

Serves 4.

Roasting and peeling fresh green chilies is much easier than you might imagine. Plus, the heady scent of the blackened skins with the moist chili cooking underneath is worth the minor bit of trouble this process takes. There are several methods, depending on how many chilies you plan to roast at a time.

If you are doing just 4 or 5 chilies, you can lay the whole chilies right on top of your stovetop burner. A gas burner is easier, but an electric one works fine. Cook on medium-high and use tongs to turn the chilies frequently. Watch to make sure the skin bubbles on each side of the chili. Slip the roasted chilies into a plastic bag, seal it, and let them sweat for 20 minutes. Then you can easily peel the skin off each chili using a knife. Wear gloves if they are hot chilies, or your skin may burn. If your eyes are sensitive, peel the chilies under a running cool-water faucet.

For a larger number of chilies, you can use the broiler in your oven, placing the chilies on a baking sheet and turning them several times during roasting. My favorite way to roast chilies is outside on a barbeque grill.

NATIVE BULLET SOUP

Meatballs:

1½ pounds ground beef or buffalo

1 cup fine bread crumbs

2 eggs

½ teaspoon sage

⅛ teaspoon black pepper

½ teaspoon salt

½ teaspoon dry mustard

Soup Base:

2 tablespoons vegetable oil

1 large onion, coarsely chopped

2 cloves garlic, crushed

2 tablespoons flour

8 cups beef broth

¼ cup red wine

4 large potatoes, peeled and diced

1 cup peeled and cubed fresh raw pumpkin

3 carrots, peeled and cubed

1 cup frozen corn

2 stalks celery, diced

1 teaspoon thyme

½ teaspoon ground sage

1 tablespoon chopped fresh parsley

1 14-ounce can diced stewed tomatoes, juice included

1 teaspoon salt

¼ teaspoon black pepper

Combine the meatball ingredients in a large bowl. Mix with your hands, making sure all the ingredients are well-incorporated. Form the mixture into 1½-inch balls and set aside on a plate.

Heat the oil in a large stock pot over medium-high heat. Sauté the onion and garlic until soft. Add the flour and stir for 3 minutes. Add 2 cups of the beef broth, stirring well to prevent lumps.

Add the remaining ingredients and bring the soup to a boil. Carefully drop the meatballs into the soup and cover the pot. Reduce the heat to medium-low and simmer for 20–30 minutes or until the potatoes are tender.

Serve immediately or refrigerate for up to 4 days. Serves 6–8.

At a county fair booth in Kamiah, Idaho, I overheard two Native American women debating the "right" way to make Bullet Soup. My curiosity got the best of me, and I asked, "What's Bullet Soup?" My interest was genuine and respectful, so these two older Nez Perce women began to tell me how to make Bullet Soup, with me writing down directions as fast as I could on the back of a checkbook.

Bullet Soup is always a meatball-studded soup with vegetables. Some tribes make it thick and heavy with the potatoes cooked until they fall apart; others prepare a lighter soup with a greater variety of ingredients like squash, corn, and tomatoes. Bullet Soups are frequently seasoned with sage and thyme. This recipe is my version of the intriguingly named soup.

WHITE MINESTRONE

1 tablespoon olive oil

1 large onion, finely diced

8 strips smoked bacon, browned, patted dry, and broken into bits

2 cups dried Cannelli beans (tiny white beans), soaked in water overnight and drained

8 cups chicken broth

2 stalks celery, diced

2 carrots, peeled and diced

1 large potato, peeled and diced into small $1/2$-inch cubes

1 green bell pepper, seeded and diced

4 cloves garlic, crushed

1 cup white wine

$3/4$ teaspoon rosemary

$3/4$ teaspoon thyme

$3/4$ teaspoon basil

$3/4$ teaspoon oregano

$1/8$ teaspoon freshly grated nutmeg

3 cups chopped fresh spinach leaves, loosely packed

freshly grated Parmesan cheese and nutmeg for garnish

In a large stock pot over medium-high heat, sauté the onion in the olive oil for 5 minutes. Add the bacon and the pre-soaked beans to the pot. Cover with the chicken broth. Bring to a boil, cover, and simmer for 30 minutes. Check the beans: they should be firm but just beginning to get tender. If they are still quite hard, simmer longer. (Larger beans may require up to 1 hour of simmering to reach the point at which they begin to soften.)

Add the remaining ingredients except the garnish. Bring to a boil, then reduce the heat and simmer for 30 minutes or until the vegetables begin to fall apart. Add extra water if the soup gets too dry or thick.

Serve with grated Parmesan and a dusting of freshly grated nutmeg.

Serves 6.

Italian miners and laborers settled all up and down the Rockies: in Bountiful, Utah; in Grand Junction, Colorado; and up as far as Salmon Arm in British Columbia, Canada. Butte, Montana, drew a large community of Italian immigrants who came to work the copper mines. In the early 1900s, the Meaderville settlement in Butte was the site of several Italian boarding houses, like Ghella Gianino's on Montana Street and Domenica Martinallo's on Leatherwood. Many courses were served at boarding house meals, beginning with antipasto plates filled with salami, cheese, vegetables, and olives, followed by a minestrone, a pasta dish, and finally the main meat course. At least seven Italian markets did a thriving business on the streets of Meaderville, making sure Italian cooks had all the staples they needed. Shoppers could get locally made salami, blood sausage, and prosciutto; cheeses and spices were imported from Italy.

A reminder of simple Italian kitchens throughout this region, this rich white minestrone is a comforting meal with bread and a salad.

Low Fat

SCANDINAVIAN BERRY-FRUIT SOUP WITH CINNAMON

2 cups pitted, halved plums

2 cups pitted, halved apricots

3 apples, peeled, cored, and cubed—
　any tart variety

3 cups fresh berries—a single type or a
　combination of strawberries, raspberries,
　huckleberries, etc.

6 cups water

$^1/_2$ cup honey

1 cinnamon stick

$^1/_4$ teaspoon vanilla

1 tablespoon fresh lemon juice

$1^1/_2$ tablespoons cornstarch dissolved in
　$^1/_4$–$^1/_2$ cup water

toast triangles with their crusts removed,
　sprinkled with a mix of 1 teaspoon
　cinnamon and 5 tablespoons white sugar

In a large saucepan, combine all the ingredients except the cornstarch and toast. Stir and bring to a boil over medium-high heat. Reduce the heat and cover the pan. Simmer for about 20 minutes or until the fruit is very soft.

Remove the pot from the heat. Purée the soup in a blender or food processor or press it through a fine sieve. Return it to the pot over the heat and stir in the cornstarch. Bring to boil again and simmer for 3–5 minutes, stirring constantly, until the soup is smooth and thickened.

Cool the soup in the refrigerator. Serve chilled with the toast triangles. Excellent as a first course or an afternoon treat.

Serves 6–8.

My Grandma Marie Kujawa Mares grew up in Libby, Montana, near the Canadian border. The residents of this scenic logging community were predominantly Scandinavian. Grandma always talked about having cold fruit soup at the kitchen tables of her childhood friends. (Since Grandma came from French Canadian and German heritage, she had to count on her friends for this treat.)

Libby is in a mountainous, piney wood setting with a wealth of fruit growing nearby, so Grandma's friends served fruit soup with everything from plums and apples to strawberries, raspberries, and huckleberries. You can get pretty wild with your fruit combinations in this refreshing summer soup. In the winter, dried fruits like raisins, dried apricots, and dried apples are tasty substitutions. Just pour boiling water over the dried fruits, let them sit for 20 minutes or until they're soft, and drain off the water.

BACON-LENTIL SOUP AU VIN

2 tablespoons extra virgin olive oil

3 cloves garlic, crushed

1 medium onion, diced

6 slices smoked bacon, browned and patted dry

2 cups dry lentils

2 carrots, peeled and diced

2 stalks celery, diced

6 cups beef broth

2 cups full-bodied red wine—like Zinfandel or Cabernet

1 teaspoon dried thyme

¼ teaspoon ground sage

½ teaspoon dried rosemary

1 teaspoon dried parsley

crusty French bread, cut into triangles, buttered, and browned in a 375° oven

In a stock pot over medium heat, sauté the garlic and onion in the olive oil. Add all the remaining ingredients (except the bread) and bring to a boil. Cover the pot, lower the heat, and simmer for 40 minutes or until the lentils are soft. You may need to add some water if the soup becomes too thick.

Serve immediately, garnished with triangles of crusty French bread, or refrigerate for up to 5 days and reheat. For a vegetarian meal, omit the bacon and add a dash of smoke flavoring.

Serves 6.

Adding wine to food creates an elusive touch of sweet or salty, woodsy or fruity, yeasty or refined character that you can only describe as being something different, something special. It's a good idea to follow this rule: never cook with a wine that isn't good to drink. Cooking wines (often found next to the vinegars on grocery store shelves) have salt added to them to make them undrinkable and therefore unusable for cooking, in my mind. Play around with adding wines to your favorite recipes. Wine in cooking mirrors the flavor of salt on the tongue; it's excellent for those on a low-sodium diet who find their food lacks flavor. Cooking with wine can even work for those who don't wish to consume alcohol: the alcohol content in wines is cooked away in less than 2 minutes of simmering.

Low Fat

BEER BREAD SOUP WITH CABBAGE

1 tablespoon extra virgin olive oil
1 large onion, diced
2 cloves garlic, crushed
5 cups chicken broth
2 cups finely chopped cabbage
3 tablespoons tomato paste
1 cup flat beer—preferably an ale
1 teaspoon sugar

$1/2$ teaspoon salt
$1/4$ teaspoon pepper
$1/8$ teaspoon cayenne pepper
1 teaspoon crushed rosemary
1 teaspoon crushed dried parsley
8 slices French or dense, crusty bread, cubed and toasted lightly to dry

freshly grated Parmesan or Romano cheese for garnish

Heat the olive oil in a soup pot over medium heat. Sauté the onion and garlic until they turn golden. Add the remaining ingredients except the bread and cheese. Bring to a boil, cover, and simmer for 20 minutes.

Divide the bread cubes among 4 soup bowls, lining the bottom of each bowl with bread. Ladle soup over the bread and garnish with grated Parmesan or Romano cheese. Serve immediately.

Serves 4.

Bread soup is an Italian tradition. I've added beer to this version because I like the yeasty, slightly bitter flavor it adds to this simple peasant soup.

The most flavorful version of this soup uses a honey nut brown ale, but do some experimenting of your own. Vegetarians can use vegetable broth instead of chicken broth for an equally satisfying soup.

TRAPPER'S BEEF JERKY SOUP

3 tablespoons olive oil

1 medium onion, coarsely chopped

2 stalks celery, diced

1 cup fresh sliced mushrooms

1½ cups chopped wild game jerky or store-bought beef jerky, presoaked in hot water for 1 hour and drained

2 cups shredded cabbage

2 carrots, diced

2 medium potatoes, peeled and cubed

2 cups sliced green beans

⅓ cup barley

½ teaspoon crushed red pepper flakes

1 teaspoon oregano

1 teaspoon rosemary

1 teaspoon thyme

1 teaspoon basil

¼ teaspoon black pepper

1 14-ounce can diced stewed tomatoes, juice included

3 cups beef broth

3 cups water

Heat the olive oil in a large stock pot over medium heat. Sauté the onion, celery, and mushrooms until soft.

Add the remaining ingredients and simmer, covered, for about 45 minutes.

Serve with biscuits or dumplings.

I demonstrated this soup on a Rocky Mountain gourmet cooking program I used to do for KRTV, a local television channel in Great Falls, Montana. I always invited people to write to me if they wanted a printed copy of a recipe. This particular recipe got a lot of interest. I'd come up with this soup off the top of my head one day while brainstorming all the ingredients that most seemed like the Rockies to me. But after I said on my cooking program that I'd made this recipe up myself, I received several letters admonishing me not to "take credit for such an old way of making soup around these parts." I guess it just goes to show there really is no such thing as an original recipe.

CHICKEN AND WHITE BEAN CHILI WITH SHOEPEG CORN

1 tablespoon vegetable oil

1 large onion, chopped

2 cloves garlic, crushed

1 green bell pepper, seeded and chopped

8 cups chicken broth

2 cups dry Great Northern beans, soaked overnight and drained

$\frac{1}{2}$ teaspoon red pepper flakes

$\frac{1}{2}$ teaspoon oregano

2 teaspoons ground cumin

1 teaspoon chili powder

1 teaspoon salt

$\frac{1}{4}$ teaspoon black pepper

2 cups diced cooked white chicken meat

1 14-ounce can white shoepeg corn

2 7-ounce cans diced green chilies

1 tablespoon cornstarch dissolved in $\frac{1}{4}$ cup water

fresh cilantro leaves and red pepper flakes for garnish

Heat the oil in a large stock pot over medium heat. Sauté the onion, garlic, and bell pepper until wilted. Do not brown.

Add the broth, beans, pepper flakes, oregano, cumin, chili powder, salt, and pepper. Bring to a boil. Cover, reduce the heat, and let simmer for 45 minutes or until the beans are tender.

Add the chicken, corn, chilies, and dissolved cornstarch. Simmer for 5 minutes more.

Garnish with fresh cilantro leaves and more red pepper flakes if desired.

Serves 8.

I grew up skiing at Showdown Ski Area near Neihart, Montana. My dad ran the ski school there. It's about the most unpretentious ski hill I've ever been on. I would never have thought of it as an appropriate place for anything gourmet (even with my constantly evolving concept of gourmet). But then I took my daughter Tessa back to Showdown so my dad could teach her to ski. While Dad did his teaching thing, I stopped to warm up at a new little hut on the hill and enjoyed a bowl of the most gourmet chili I'd ever tasted. It was a white bean chicken chili, made by a part-time cook and fly-fishing guide (you can do that in Montana) named Johnny Kowalski. By the time Tessa and Dad made it in for their warm-up, I was jotting down every ingredient I could detect in Johnny's chili. When I tried the recipe at home, I was pretty pleased with it.

Low Fat

ELK AND BLACK BEAN CHILI

2 tablespoons olive oil

1 pound elk steak, trimmed and cut into cubes

1 large onion, diced

2 cloves garlic, crushed

3 cups dry black beans, presoaked overnight and drained

1 whole bay leaf

6 cups water

1 large green bell pepper, seeded and diced

2 28-ounce cans stewed tomatoes, broken into pieces, with their juice

4 cups beef broth

2 14-ounce cans tomato sauce

4 tablespoons brown sugar

1 7-ounce can diced green chilies

6 tablespoons chili powder

2 tablespoons ground cumin

$1/4$ teaspoon cinnamon

$1/2$ teaspoon ground coriander

$1/8$ teaspoon ground cloves

2 tablespoons cocoa powder

$1/2$–1 teaspoon cayenne pepper, to taste

1 cup red wine

pine nuts for garnish

Heat the olive oil in a large stock pot over medium-high heat. Sauté the elk meat until it browns. Add the onion and garlic and sauté for another 5 minutes.

Add the black beans, bay leaf, and water. Bring to a boil. Cover the pot, reduce the heat, and simmer for $1^1/_2$ hours.

Add the remaining ingredients (except the pine nuts) and simmer for another 30–45 minutes, until the beans are tender. You may need to add more water if the chili becomes too thick.

Serve garnished with pine nuts.

Serves 8–10.

I love to cook with elk meat, as much for the delicious flavor and tender texture of the meat as for the tradition (it goes back for generations in my family) of providing food for the table in this way. Cooking with elk always conjures up memories of elk hunting on horseback with my dad. I'm proud of the fact that I rarely even ate beef as a child, because it was too expensive and my dad hunted for our meat. This special elk chili recipe, with elk steak cubes instead of the more commonly used ground meat, does the elk species proud in my opinion.

CURRIED ALMOND RICE SOUP

2 tablespoons butter
½ cup finely diced onion
½ cup finely diced celery
½ cup finely diced carrot
1 clove garlic, crushed
1 cup long-grained white rice
5 cups chicken or vegetable broth
¼ cup sherry
½ teaspoon thyme
¾ teaspoon salt
1 teaspoon hot curry powder
¼ teaspoon black pepper

1 cup finely slivered almonds
1 cup half-and-half

Melt the butter in a medium-sized soup pot over medium heat. Sauté the onion, celery, carrot, and garlic for 5 minutes.

Add the remaining ingredients except the almonds and half-and-half. Stir well and bring to boil. Then cover the pot, reduce the heat, and simmer for 30 minutes.

Add the almonds and half-and-half and simmer for another 5 minutes. Serve immediately.

Serves 4.

I try to prepare meals with varied and lively flavors that oppose as well as complement each other in texture and color. The menu below does exactly that. The soup can be made a day ahead; so can parts of the salad, with final assembly just before serving. The dessert is weird and wonderful and bound to jump-start one's tastebuds.

Suggested Menu:
- Curried Almond Rice Soup
- Asian Pheasant, Cabbage, and Spinach Salad with Sesame Dressing (page 43)
- Spiced Banana Egg Rolls with Frozen Yogurt (page 122) and Cowboy Coffee Sauce (page 123)
- Gerwürtztraminer Wine

Low Fat

ZUCCHINI-BUTTERMILK SOUP

1 teaspoon canola oil

½ cup diced onion

4 cups chopped zucchini, cut it into 1-inch cubes with the peel left on

2 stalks celery, diced

1 clove garlic, crushed

1 large potato, peeled and cubed

2 teaspoons cornstarch

3 cups chicken or vegetable broth

2 tablespoons sherry

⅛ teaspoon marjoram

¼ teaspoon curry

½ teaspoon salt

1 teaspoon minced fresh mint

1 cup nonfat or lowfat buttermilk

fresh chives and/or Hungarian paprika for garnish

In a medium-sized saucepan over medium heat, sauté the onion in the oil for 5 minutes.

Add the remaining ingredients except the buttermilk and garnish. Bring to a boil. Cover the pan, lower the heat, and simmer for 20 minutes, stirring occasionally.

Purée the soup in a food processor or blender in four batches. Return it to the pot and add the buttermilk. Heat gently to serving temperature—do not boil. Sprinkle with fresh chives and/or Hungarian paprika and serve immediately.

To prepare ahead, complete all steps except the addition of the buttermilk and refrigerate for up to 2 days. Add the buttermilk just before serving and reheat carefully.

Serves 4.

"You know, those city folks have to lock their cars up tighter than a drum to keep someone from stealing their radio, or even driving away with the whole damn car, but around _____ [insert name of any small town with a population of less than 2,000] we have to lock up our cars just to keep the neighbors from filling our backseats with giant homegrown zucchini."

As most small-town residents know, this zucchini-leaving story is not a joke. Now that I live in a bigger town, I'd give anything to have people filling up my car with garden-fresh zucchini. However, I'd be tempted to leave a polite note requesting that the zucchini bandits donate only the vegetables under six inches in length. The giant ones have seeds that could break a tooth.

This recipe is a refreshing and surprisingly light soup that is best prepared with the smallest zucchini you can get your hands on.

Low Fat

TROUT IN LEMON BROTH WITH PEAS

1 cup sliced white mushrooms

¼ cup diced scallions

1 clove garlic, crushed

½ cup diced red bell pepper

4 cups chicken or vegetable broth

1 cup white wine

juice of 2 fresh lemons

1 teaspoon grated fresh ginger root

½ teaspoon salt

1 teaspoon hot pepper sauce, Louisiana pepper sauce, Tabasco, or jalapeño sauce

1 tablespoon soy sauce

1½ cups flaked baked trout, in 1-inch pieces

1 cup frozen or fresh petite green peas

finely slivered almonds for garnish

In a medium-sized soup pot over medium heat, combine all the ingredients except the trout, peas, and almonds. Increase heat to medium-high and bring to a boil, stirring well to blend the flavors. Reduce the heat and simmer for 5 minutes, uncovered.

Carefully add the trout and peas and let them gently simmer for just 1 minute, until heated through.

Ladle into serving bowls and garnish with slivered almonds.

Serves 4.

Fishing enthusiasts go around and around about the best fish for eating—pike, trout, perch, bass. All I can say is that if I'm going to go to a wild spot and stand thigh-deep in the river, begging a wily trout to jump at the caddis fly I've so carefully chosen to fit its tastes, then I feel I owe it to that trout to do my best job serving it in its most pristine glory. This soup is an elegant way to prepare trout, with only fresh flavors to complement the freshwater quality of this fine-textured fish. But when all the niceties of your kitchen aren't available—say you're 20 miles from nowhere, fishing a high-mountain lake—a piece of foil, a fire or camp stove, and some salt and pepper are the perfect preparation for this precious wild food.

SALADS

Bavarian Red Potato and Apple Salad

Jicama Citrus Salad with Red Peppers

Wheat Berry Salad with Grapes and Asparagus

Asian Pheasant, Cabbage, and Spinach Salad with Sesame Dressing

Thai Elk Salad with Lime Marinade

Avocado Boats with Balsamic Vinegar–Olive Oil Marinade

Wild Rice, Pear, and White Bean Salad with Honey–Sage Dressing

Warm Dandelion Salad with Mushrooms, Walnuts, and Parmesan

Warm Black Bean Salad with Cinnamon Dressing

Salad Dressings:

Balsamic Vinaigrette

Nonfat Rosehip Yogurt Dressing

Wild Huckleberry Dressing

Low Fat

BAVARIAN RED POTATO AND APPLE SALAD

2 tablespoons vegetable oil

$\frac{1}{2}$ cup chopped onion

2 stalks celery, diced

1 dash smoke flavoring
(must be less than $\frac{1}{16}$ teaspoon)

2 teaspoons all-purpose flour

4 teaspoons sugar

$\frac{1}{2}$ teaspoon salt

$\frac{1}{4}$ teaspoon celery seed

$\frac{1}{8}$ teaspoon freshly ground black pepper

$\frac{1}{2}$ cup apple juice or cider

$\frac{1}{4}$ cup water

2 tablespoons balsamic vinegar or
3 tablespoons cider vinegar

$1\frac{1}{2}$ pounds red-skinned potatoes, cubed, boiled
until just tender, and drained

2 Granny Smith apples, cored and cubed
(do not peel)

In large skillet, heat the oil and sauté the onion, celery, and smoke flavoring over medium-high heat until the vegetables are tender. Stir in the flour and cook for 1 minute to dissolve well. Whisk in the sugar, salt, celery seed, pepper, juice, water, and vinegar. Cook for about 5 minutes more until the mixture is smooth and thickened. Stir in the potatoes and apples and cook until heated through, about 2 minutes more. Serve warm.

Serves 4.

German settlers have felt at home in the Rocky Mountains since the mid-1800s. This is a lighter recipe for the usually bacon-grease-laden German potato salad (which I adore) with a smoky sweet-tart flavor. The combination of apples and red potatoes in my salad isn't far off the mark, since mashed potatoes with apple sauce (called *Himmel und Erde*) is a common Bavarian side dish. This salad is a healthy complement to the less heart-healthy but still-delicious grilled German-style Wurst sausages.

JICAMA CITRUS SALAD WITH RED PEPPERS

4 cups peeled, cut fresh jicama, cut in julienne strips (about 2 large jicama tubers)

1 red bell pepper, sliced into 2-inch-long thin strips

4 scallions, diced

juice of 1 fresh lime

1/2 teaspoon salt

1/4 cup coarsely chopped cilantro leaves

1 orange, peeled and sliced into 1/2-inch chunks

1/4–1/2 teaspoon red pepper flakes

1/4 teaspoon freshly ground pepper

1/2 clove garlic, crushed

2 tablespoons vegetable oil

Combine all the ingredients in a large bowl, stirring to coat well. Cover and refrigerate for at least 1/2 hour before serving.

This salad may be stored in the refrigerator for up to 8 hours before being served. You can also prepare all the ingredients a full day ahead, storing the sliced vegetables separately from the remaining ingredients, and combine within the last hour before serving.

Serves 4.

A crisp, sweet, turnip-shaped southwestern root vegetable, jicama is quite easy to find year-round in the gourmet vegetable section of your market or with the potatoes. I enjoy the jicama's texture and flavor so much, I decided it should star in its own salad.

Place clean spinach leaves on a salad plate, and arrange the jicama salad in the center of the spinach. This makes a lively presentation, perfect for a summer meal on the front porch accompanied by fresh lime margaritas.

WHEAT BERRY SALAD WITH GRAPES AND ASPARAGUS

3 cups water, more if necessary

¼ teaspoon salt

½ cup wheat berries

½ cup diced scallions

1 pound fresh asparagus spears, sliced in thirds and steamed for 3 minutes

1 cup red seedless grapes

¼ cup coarsely chopped walnuts

1 teaspoon sesame oil

3 tablespoons vegetable oil

4 tablespoons soy sauce

1 tablespoon Chinese mustard

5 tablespoons rice wine vinegar

1 tablespoon balsamic vinegar

1 tablespoon grated fresh ginger root

4 cups loosely packed spinach leaves, cleaned, dried, and hand ripped

Bring the water, salt, and wheat berries to a boil in a small saucepan. Simmer on low heat, uncovered, for 45 minutes to an hour, until the wheat is tender. Stir occasionally and add more water if necessary. Drain the wheat in a sieve when done.

Stir the remaining ingredients (except the spinach) into the wheat until all ingredients are well incorporated. Lay the spinach leaves in the bottom of a salad bowl or divide them among the salad plates. Spoon the wheat salad on top. Serve immediately, slightly warm or at room temperature.

To prepare ahead, combine the cooked wheat, scallions, asparagus, grapes, and walnuts in one bowl and the remaining ingredients (except spinach) in another. Combine the contents of the two bowls 10 minutes before serving. Arrange the spinach under the salad as above.

Serves 4-6

Serve this salad with Sea Bass in Cashew Crust with Gingered Apricot Sauce (page 108) for a lovely springtime-in-the-Rockies menu.

ASIAN PHEASANT, CABBAGE, AND SPINACH SALAD WITH SESAME DRESSING

Salad:

- 2 cups sliced roasted pheasant breast, sliced in strips
- 3 cups shredded cabbage—use half red and half green
- 1 cup shredded carrot
- 4 cups lightly packed fresh spinach leaves
- ¼ cup scallions, diced
- ½ cup celery, diced
- 1 cup sliced red bell pepper, cut into 2-inch strips
- ½ cup slivered almonds
- 1 cup quartered mushrooms

Dressing:

- ¼ cup soy sauce
- 2 tablespoons Chinese mustard
- 4 tablespoons rice wine vinegar
- 2 tablespoons honey
- 2 tablespoons sesame oil
- ⅛ cup orange juice
- 1 tablespoon grated fresh ginger root
- ⅛ teaspoon cayenne pepper

toasted sesame seeds for garnish

Combine the first set of ingredients in a large bowl.

Whisk the dressing ingredients together and pour over the salad just before serving. Toss well. Garnish with toasted sesame seeds.

Serves 4-6.

During a fundraiser for a local chapter of Pheasants Forever, a conservation organization dedicated to preservation of wild-pheasant populations and habitats, a conversation about pheasant recipes spawned the creation of this tasty salad.

To cook this wild delicacy, err on the side of undercooking. Don't worry about making sure there is no pink left in the meat. Pheasant is even leaner than chicken and toughens tremendously when overcooked. Pheasant pieces will roast in 30–40 minutes and a whole bird in an hour.

Low Fat

THAI ELK SALAD WITH LIME MARINADE

Elk and Marinade:

1½ pounds elk tenderloin
    juice of 1 lime
2 cloves garlic
3 tablespoons soy sauce

Salad:

8 ounces rice noodles, prepared according to package directions and drained
½ cup sliced celery
2 jalapeño peppers, minced, with seeds
4 cups firmly packed ripped spinach leaves
2 cups shredded carrot

2 small cucumbers, sliced in rounds and then in half-moon shapes
¼ cup fresh cilantro leaves, minced

Dressing:

2 tablespoons sesame oil
⅛ cup soy sauce
⅛ cup rice wine vinegar
    juice of 1 lime
⅛ teaspoon cayenne pepper
4 tablespoons Dijon mustard
1 tablespoon grated fresh ginger root

Combine the marinade ingredients and pour over the elk meat. Marinate for at least 4 hours and up to 1 day.

Pour off the marinade, and roast for 25 minutes in a preheated 400° oven (for rare meat, cook 8 minutes less, for well done meat, cook 10–15 minutes longer).

Slice the cooked elk into strips and combine with the salad ingredients. Whisk together the dressing ingredients, pour over the salad, and toss well.

Serves 6.

Even though I've grown up surrounded by family and friends who hunt, I've never known anyone as inspiring—almost spiritually so—on the subject of North America's hunting heritage as Jim Posewitz. The author of *Beyond Fair Chase: The Ethic and Tradition of Hunting,* Posewitz has a contagious enthusiasm for preserving the hunting way of life, respectfully paired with a strong commitment to the conservation of wild animals and their habitat.

Posewitz, who created Orion-The Hunters Institute, invited me to one of the group's wild game potluck dinners. It was one of the most overwhelming culinary feasts I'd ever participated in. The buffet table at the historic Montana Club in Helena, Montana, was covered with such delicacies as smoked elk in currant sauce, pheasant in apple-huckleberry marinade, trout baked with lemon and dill, and venison in sherried mushroom sauce over noodles. It was that Orion dinner that really jump-started my craziest and tastiest experiments in cooking with wild game.

AVOCADO BOATS WITH BALSAMIC VINEGAR–OLIVE OIL MARINADE

½ cup extra virgin olive oil

½ cup balsamic vinegar

1 clove garlic, crushed

¼ teaspoon salt

¼ teaspoon freshly ground black pepper

4 ripe avocados

¼ pound whole fresh spinach leaves

freshly grated Asiago cheese for garnish

Combine the olive oil, vinegar, garlic, salt, and pepper in a small mixing bowl and whisk thoroughly.

Cut each avocado in half lengthwise and remove the seed.

Arrange the spinach leaves on four salad plates and place two avocado halves on each plate. Pour marinade into the seed hollow of each half avocado. Grate Asiago cheese directly over each plate and serve immediately.

Serves 4.

This is by far one of the simplest salad preparations I make. It's almost embarrassing to call it a recipe. Regardless, this way of serving avocado is delicious, and it's easy to prepare when you've had a busy day and want something more than a broiled chicken breast or fish fillet on your dinner table.

WILD RICE, PEAR, AND WHITE BEAN SALAD WITH HONEY-SAGE DRESSING

Salad:

- ½ cup uncooked wild rice
- 1½ cups water
- 2 cups freshly cooked or canned, drained white navy beans
- ½ cup diced celery
- ¼ cup diced scallions
- 2 ripe Bosc pears, sliced in cubes

Dressing:

- 4 tablespoons extra virgin olive oil
- 1 tablespoon stone-ground mustard
- 3 tablespoons apple cider vinegar
- 1 tablespoon balsamic vinegar
- 3 tablespoons honey
- ½ teaspoon rubbed sage
- ½ teaspoon salt
- ¼ teaspoon freshly ground black pepper

Combine the wild rice and water in a small saucepan. Bring to a boil, cover, and reduce heat to medium-low. Simmer until the rice is tender, about 45 minutes. Cool the rice completely and refrigerate.

Mix the cooled rice with the white beans, celery, scallions, and pears. Whisk the remaining ingredients together and pour over the rice mixture, stirring to distribute dressing well. Serve immediately.

You can prepare this salad up to 1 day ahead by completing all the steps except the addition of the pears. Add the pears just before serving.

Serves 4.

Photographer, author, mountain-bike guru, and Colorado resident Dennis Coello told me about an ingenious use of wild sage once. Coello is one of those people who thinks nothing of loading his bike with the basics and heading off on a 2,000 mile trip. Usually, he travels with tortillas and peanut butter in his pack. Coello explained that after becoming bored with eating the same old thing several days in a row during one of his extra-long bike treks, he picked some wild sage, rubbed it between his hands to break up the leaves and release their flavor, and sprinkled the herb on his peanut butter-slathered tortilla. This earthy snack has become one of his mountain-biking staples. I think about Coello whenever I prepare a recipe with sage like this one.

Warm Dandelion Salad with Mushrooms, Walnuts, and Parmesan

3 tablespoons extra virgin olive oil

1 clove garlic, crushed

¼ cup finely diced red onion

½ pound fresh mushrooms, sliced—use a variety of porcini, morel, or enoki, if desired

¼ cup apple cider

4 tablespoons white or red wine vinegar

1 tablespoon balsamic vinegar

2 tablespoons honey

1½ teaspoons corn starch

½ teaspoon salt

½ teaspoon black pepper

¼ cup walnuts, hand-broken into pieces

1 pound tender, young dandelion greens, washed and trimmed

½ cup freshly grated Parmesan cheese

strips of red bell pepper for garnish

Heat the olive oil in a skillet over medium heat. Sauté the garlic, onion, and mushrooms for 5 minutes.

While these ingredients are cooking, combine the apple cider, vinegars, honey, corn starch, salt, and pepper in a cup, stirring to blend. Pour this liquid into the sauté pan after the 5 minutes is up and stir constantly until thickened—about 3 more minutes. Remove from heat and let cool slightly.

Combine the walnuts, dandelion greens, and Parmesan cheese in a large salad bowl. Drizzle the warm dressing over the greens and toss well. Garnish with strips of red bell pepper.

Serves 4.

When I was a home economics student at The University of Montana in Missoula, National Public Radio contributor and naturalist Kim Williams came to most of the home economics department receptions and evening seminars.

Twice a month, Kim shared her adventures in gathering, cooking, and eating wild plants on *All Things Considered*, and she wrote about similar topics for the *Missoulian* newspaper. I loved hearing her talk about all the ways to cook and use dandelions, and actually became a cautious dandelion convert. (My tight college food budget may have had something to do with it.) In Kim's book *Eating Wild Plants*, she explained that by using only the earliest spring dandelions, you can avoid the bitter taste usually associated with this plant. It's also important to choose leaves from plants that have no flower buds. Surprisingly, if you see even a few flowers in a field of dandelions, it's a sure bet that all of the dandelion greens in that field will have reached the bitter stage.

WARM BLACK BEAN SALAD WITH CINNAMON DRESSING

Salad:

  2 cups dried black beans, rinsed, soaked overnight, and drained
  1 small yellow onion, diced
  2 stalks celery, diced
  2 cloves garlic, crushed
 $1/2$ teaspoon cinnamon
 $1/4$ teaspoon cayenne pepper
  1 teaspoon salt

Dressing:

 $1/2$ cup diced scallion
 $1/2$ cup diced red bell pepper
 $1/4$ cup extra virgin olive oil
  3 tablespoons honey
 $1/4$ teaspoon cinnamon
 $1/4$ teaspoon cayenne pepper
 $1/8$ teaspoon freshly ground black pepper
 $1/2$ teaspoon salt
  juice of 1 lemon
  5 tablespoons balsamic vinegar

Put the soaked beans in a large stock pot. Add water to at least 2 inches above the level of the beans. Add the onion, celery, garlic, cinnamon, cayenne, and salt. Heat to boiling, then reduce the heat to low and simmer, covered, for $1–1^1/2$ hours or until the beans are tender but not falling apart. (You may need to add additional water to keep the beans covered.) Remove from heat, cool partially, then drain the liquid off.

Combine the dressing ingredients and toss with the warm beans. Serve immediately. The salad can also be refrigerated and reheated for serving up to 24 hours after the dressing is added.

Serves 6–8.

After meeting Elizabeth Berry at the Santa Fe, New Mexico, farmers' market one October, I became excited about the heady variety of legumes (otherwise known as dry beans) available for use in cooking up robust pots of frijoles. Berry, a famous organic gardener who's been featured in magazine and newspaper articles nationwide, is known most especially for her beans. Her home and garden, called Gallina Canyon Ranch, are in north central New Mexico, just north of Abiquiu, near artist Georgia O'Keefe's Ghost Ranch retreat.

Berry has a fun little bean catalog depicting each of her heirloom bean varieties in drawings—spots or no spots; shaped like eggs or caterpillars; brown, red, white, black, or combinations of the colors.

BALSAMIC VINAIGRETTE

¼ cup Dijon mustard

4 tablespoons honey

¼ cup balsamic vinegar

¼ cup rice wine vinegar

1 clove garlic, crushed

⅓ cup extra virgin olive oil

1 teaspoon dried thyme leaves or
2 teaspoons fresh thyme leaves

1 teaspoon salt

2 tablespoons fresh-squeezed lemon juice

¼ teaspoon freshly ground black pepper

4 green onions, finely minced,
green tops included

Combine all the ingredients in a jar or container with a lid and shake well. This dressing is best made at least 2 hours before serving so the flavors have a chance to blend. Shake again prior to dressing your salad. Keeps well in the refrigerator for up to 10 days.

During a quick stop at the graceful and charming Hotel Saint Francis in downtown Santa Fe, New Mexico, I first experienced the deep, rich taste of balsamic vinegar. I was taking in the elaborate sights, scents, and sounds of the annual Fiesta on the Plaza. I had ordered a light salad with baby spinach leaves as a respite from all the fiery chilies I'd been consuming. My wimpy Montana tastebuds needed a bit of cooling, sweet comfort. Balsamic vinegar, a reduction of red wine vinegar that originated in Modena, Italy, became a common addition to my recipes after that day.

Low Fat

NONFAT ROSEHIP YOGURT DRESSING

½ cup orange juice

4 tablespoons rosehip powder

2 cups plain nonfat yogurt

4 tablespoons honey

2 tablespoons stone-ground mustard

½ teaspoon salt

1 teaspoon finely grated ginger root

½ teaspoon dried thyme or 1 teaspoon fresh thyme

⅛ teaspoon cayenne pepper

¼ teaspoon freshly ground black pepper

Combine the orange juice and rosehip powder in a small saucepan over medium heat. Whisk until bubbly and thickened. Remove from heat and pour into a sealable container to cool.

When the orange-rosehip mixture has cooled, whisk in the remaining ingredients until well incorporated. Refrigerate for at least 2 hours to allow the flavors to blend before serving. This dressing will keep for up to 7 days in the refrigerator.

Once rosehips have dried on wild rosebushes, they are very easy to pick. Collect the rosehips, then let them air dry until all of the moisture has evaporated and the hips are hard and shrivelled. You can lay the hips in a single layer on a cookie sheet and place it in a 175° oven for 4–6 hours to speed the drying process. Once dry, purée the hips in a coffee bean grinder to a powdered form. Store in an air-tight container in a dark cupboard to preserve the high vitamin C content.

WILD HUCKLEBERRY DRESSING

¹/₂ cup fresh or frozen huckleberries, mashed
with a spoon, or ¹/₃ cup bottled
huckleberry juice

¹/₄ cup water

¹/₂ cup good-quality red wine vinegar

 1 tablespoon balsamic vinegar

¹/₂ cup canola oil

³/₄ teaspoon salt

 2 tablespoons Dijon mustard

¹/₄ teaspoon freshly ground black pepper

dash of red chili pepper sauce like Tabasco

Combine all the ingredients in a jar or plastic container with a lid and shake well. Serve immediately or refrigerate for up to 10 days.

Around Seeley Lake, Montana, and in other hot spots in the Northern Rockies, you have to beat the bears to the berries; sometimes it can be a close call. I've found that my constantly chattering daughter Tessa seems to ward off huckleberry-crazed bears better than any bear bell. In my family, we consider it a point of pride to have a freezer full of huckleberries to dole out for muffins, jams, sauces, and an occasional pie. (I'm rarely enticed into making a pie because pies use entirely too much of my berry stash in one dessert.) As you can see, I'm rather stingy with my huckleberries. I adore using them in this salad dressing, since it can stretch the taste of my berries out over several meals.

GRAINS, LEGUMES, PASTAS, AND VEGETABLES

Asparagus with Toasted Hazelnuts and Garlic

Root Vegetables Au Gratin with Nutmeg

Confetti Corn

Ginger- and Cherry-Glazed Pumpkin

Basque Green Beans in Tomato Broth

Stuffed Vegetables with Pine Nuts

Petite Peas with Prosciutto and Garlic

Feta- and Lemon-Crumb Stuffed Artichokes

Oriental Noodles with Tofu and Peanut Sauce

Steamed Carrots and Zucchini with Chipotle Chili Butter

Corn and Pepper Cakes

Warm Balsamic Frijole Salad

Wild Mushroom and Walnut Bread Pudding with Jarlsberg

Nutmeg Spätzle

Spiced Red Risotto

Dried Apple and Walnut Quinoa

Green Chili Penne Pasta with Cilantro and Pine Nuts

Au Gratin Potatoes with Horseradish

Sweet Potato Hash Browns with Jalepeño and Red Onion

Green Chili Gnocchi

Cilantro Pesto

Chili-Orange Oil

ASPARAGUS WITH TOASTED HAZELNUTS AND GARLIC

 ½ cup shelled hazelnuts
 4 tablespoons butter
 3 cloves garlic, slivered
 2 tablespoons dry sherry
 ¼ cup apple juice
 ½ teaspoon salt
 ¼ teaspoon freshly ground black pepper
 1 pound of thin (¼ inch or less in diameter) asparagus, ends trimmed

 minced red bell pepper for garnish

Place a skillet on the stovetop over medium-high heat. Toast the hazelnuts, stirring constantly, until they begin to turn brown. Pour the nuts into a small bowl.

Return the skillet to the heat. Melt the butter and add the slivered garlic. Stir, watching closely, until the garlic turns light brown on the edges. Add the sherry, apple juice, salt, and pepper. Simmer for 2–3 minutes, until the alcohol cooks away. Remove the skillet from the heat.

In a large steamer basket, steam the asparagus for 3–5 minutes. They should be tender but still crisp. Immediately add the asparagus and nuts to the sauce in the skillet. Turn all the ingredients with a spatula to coat well. Garnish with minced red bell pepper.

Serves 4.

The Pacific Northwest, Santa Fe, Grand Trunk Pacific, and Canadian Pacific railroads did much for the settlement of the Rockies. Before the railroad companies were able to support themselves through freight fees, they built elegant first-class destination resorts to attract more travelers. The revenue helped pay for building the railroads.

To cater to the more refined natures of those who could afford to travel west for vacations, the railroads adopted a European style of design, cuisine, and service. Travelers from the East did not have to suffer primitive food. In fact, the dishes served in dining cars, at train stations, and at destinations like the Banff Springs Hotel in Banff, Alberta, were most often French, prepared with the finest ingredients.

When I visited the railroad museum in Livingston, Montana, I was fascinated by the formal china and the complicated menus. One of the menus for boarding passengers, printed in delicate script, included an asparagus dish that inspired this recipe.

ROOT VEGETABLES AU GRATIN WITH NUTMEG

Root Vegetables:

1 cup peeled, cubed rutabaga
1 cup peeled, cubed turnip
1 cup peeled, cubed parsnip
1 cup peeled, cubed carrot
1 cup peeled, cubed yam

Au Gratin:

1 medium onion, chopped
1/4 cup butter
2 tablespoons flour
1 teaspoon salt
1/2 teaspoon black pepper
1 1/2 cups half-and-half
1 cup whole milk
1/4 teaspoon freshly grated nutmeg
1/2 cup freshly grated Parmesan cheese

Preheat the oven to 375°. Grease a casserole or baking dish.

In a large pot of boiling salted water, parboil the root vegetables for 8 minutes. Drain well.

Melt the butter in a large saucepan and sauté the onions until they are soft. Stir in the flour, salt, and pepper. Cook for 2 minutes, stirring to dissolve. Stir in the half-and-half, milk, and nutmeg. Remove the sauce from the heat and combine with the vegetables.

Pour the mixture into the greased dish. Sprinkle the Parmesan on top. Bake uncovered for 45 minutes until brown and bubbly.

Serves 6.

In the late 1800s, Evelyn Cameron left her home in Great Britain, and she and her husband, Ewen, bought a ranch in the barren plains of eastern Montana. I've long admired a particular self-portrait of this renowned western photographer.

In the portrait, she is posed in her vegetable garden. Her arms are loaded with the vegetables she grew and sold to railroad workers, ranchers, and cowboys to supplement her income. Piled on the crusty ground below her cotton plaid apron, are squash of every shape and variety. The diversity of the squash and vegetables surprised me. I'd always imagined that the cupboards of early western settlers were filled with plain food—potatoes, wild game or beef, and the makings for biscuits.

Cameron's journals include detailed descriptions of meals, gardening techniques, berry-picking trips, and game hunting. Her 1895 records show that Cameron sold over half a ton of vegetables that year and cleared $41.20. Her journal entry on September 14, 1897 lists an impressive collection of vegetables she'd spent the day harvesting, including beans, cucumbers, cauliflower, squash, cabbage, potatoes, and onions.

CONFETTI CORN

2 tablespoons butter

6 cups corn, frozen or cut fresh from the cob

½ cup finely diced red bell pepper

½ cup finely diced green bell pepper

2 large fresh tomatoes, sliced into 1-inch cubes

¼ cup minced red onion

½ teaspoon red pepper flakes

1 clove garlic, crushed

¼ teaspoon salt

¼ teaspoon black pepper

⅛ cup minced fresh cilantro leaves

juice of one fresh lime

pine nuts and additional cilantro leaves for garnish

Melt the butter in a large frying pan over medium heat. Add all the ingredients (except the lime juice and garnish,) and toss. Stir constantly until the vegetables are heated through. This should take 3–5 minutes. The peppers and onions should still be crisp and the tomatoes firm. Remove the pan from the heat .

Squeeze the juice of 1 fresh lime over the vegetables. Garnish with pine nuts and more fresh cilantro leaves.

Serves 6–8.

Descended from the Anasazi, New Mexico's seventeen tribes of Pueblo Indians still celebrate many of the traditional Anasazi feast days. Each pueblo has its own distinctive pottery, clothing, music, and jewelry, but many celebrate similar feast days. The Corn Dance, which inspired this recipe, is one of the most common.

Low
Fat

GINGER- AND CHERRY-GLAZED PUMPKIN

$^1/_2$ cup dried cherries

$^3/_4$ cup white wine

$^1/_4$ cup honey

3 tablespoons molasses

$^1/_4$ cup orange juice

2 tablespoons grated fresh ginger

$^1/_2$ teaspoon salt

$^1/_8$ teaspoon cayenne pepper

$^1/_4$ teaspoon ground cumin

8 cups peeled fresh pumpkin,
sliced into 1-inch cubes

Preheat the oven to 350°.

In a small saucepan over medium heat, combine all the ingredients except the pumpkin. Bring to a boil, then lower the heat and simmer, stirring frequently, for 5 minutes or until the sauce begins to thicken.

Spread the pumpkin in a casserole baking dish. Pour the cherry-ginger mixture over the pumpkin cubes. Cover the casserole loosely with foil and bake for 45–60 minutes, until the pumpkin is fork tender. Baste the pumpkin with the sauce at least twice during the baking period.

Take the foil off the casserole, increase the oven temperature to 425°, and brown for a final 10 minutes.

Serves 6.

This lowfat pumpkin dish proves that more can come from a pumpkin than just a rich custard pie. Save the traditional pie for the holidays. This recipe will help you enjoy pumpkin throughout autumn.

A railroad dining stop in Evanston, Wyoming, during the 1870s and 1880s, before the luxurious dining cars came along, developed a reputation for fine food. Most of the dining stops served thin, shoe-leather steak and corn bread for every trainfull of passengers. But in Evanston, there was a menu that included pan-fried trout, fresh garden vegetables, and baked squash like this simple pumpkin dish.

BASQUE GREEN BEANS IN TOMATO BROTH

1½ pounds fresh green beans, trimmed
2 tablespoons extra virgin olive oil
3 cloves garlic, crushed
½ cup finely diced red onion
½ teaspoon basil
½ teaspoon oregano
½ teaspoon thyme
¼–1 teaspoon red pepper flakes (depending on taste)
¼ cup minced fresh parsley
1 cup V-8 style tomato juice
2 tablespoons balsamic vinegar

½ cup beef broth
½ teaspoon salt
¼ teaspoon freshly ground black pepper
2 fresh tomatoes, seeded and chopped

Bring a large pot of salted water to a rolling boil. Add the beans and cook for 5–7 minutes, until tender-crisp. Drain the beans and immediately plunge them in cold water to stop the cooking process. Set aside.

In a skillet, sauté the garlic and onion in the olive oil. Add the remaining ingredients except the beans and tomatoes. Simmer for 15 minutes. Add the beans and tomatoes and stir gently. Serve immediately.

Serves 4–6.

Immigrants from the Basque region of northern Spain came to the Rockies as sheepherders, settling in Colorado, Idaho, and Utah. The Basque way of eating features meals that go on and on—a seemingly unending array of courses. They start with platters of fresh vegetables, salami, and olives. Then comes a rich vegetable soup, pinto beans, and lots of crusty round loaves of bread. Pasta, not to mention pickled tongue and pigs feet, may take your stomach to the edge, but there's still a salad with tangy vinaigrette, a steak or roasted lamb, Basque green beans, and potatoes to come. All of this food is served with jugs of red wine and more bread.

STUFFED VEGETABLES WITH PINE NUTS

Vegetables:

- 4 small zucchini
- 4 yellow bell peppers
- 4 medium tomatoes

Stuffing:

- 2 medium onions, finely diced
- 2 cloves garlic
- 4 teaspoons extra virgin olive oil
- 1/4 teaspoon salt
- 1/4 teaspoon black pepper
- 2 cups cooked long-grain white rice

- 1/2 cup pine nuts
- 1 teaspoon basil
- 1/4 teaspoon nutmeg (freshly ground is best)
- 1/2 cup grated Romano cheese
- 1 tablespoon grated fresh lemon rind
- 1/4 cup sliced black olives

Preheat the oven to 375°.

Cut the zucchinis in half lengthwise, and cut the tops off the peppers and tomatoes. Hollow out the centers of the tomatoes and zucchinis with a melon ball scoop. Pull the seeds out of the peppers.

Combine the remaining ingredients in a mixing bowl and stir well.

Fill the vegetables with the rice stuffing. Place the zucchinis and peppers on a baking sheet and bake for 15 minutes. Add the tomatoes to the pan and continue baking for another 10–15 minutes, until the vegetables become tender. Serve immediately.

Serves 4.

My own regular diet often includes completely vegetarian meals for several days in a row, but being a true vegetarian in meat country can be a challenge. Vegetarians must feel a lot of pressure to be meat eaters in big ranching states like Montana, Wyoming, and Colorado. With a little imagination, you *can* be a graceful vegetarian in the Rockies. With the recipe I created above, you can do it with pizazz.

PETITE PEAS WITH PROSCIUTTO AND GARLIC

1 tablespoon extra virgin olive oil

3 scallions, diced

2 cloves garlic, crushed

¼ pound fresh prosciutto or browned bacon, cut into thin strips

¼ cup minced fresh basil leaves

½ teaspoon salt

¼ teaspoon freshly ground black pepper

4 cups fresh or frozen petite green peas

Heat the olive oil in a large non-stick skillet over medium-high heat. Add the scallions and garlic and sauté for 2 minutes.

Add the remaining ingredients to the pan and cook, tossing continuously, for another 3–5 minutes, just until heated through.

Serve immediately.

Serves 4–6.

Prosciutto is not an ingredient that is usually associated with the Rocky Moutains, but it is an excellent substitute for bacon in special recipes. I like to use prosciutto in this recipe with tiny peas from the garden, because its deep pink color is a more elegant complement to the green of this fresh vegetable than browned bacon is.

FETA- AND LEMON-CRUMB STUFFED ARTICHOKES

Stuffing:

- 5 tablespoons olive oil
- 1 clove garlic, crushed
- 1/4 cup freshly grated Parmesan cheese
- 3/4 cup fine bread crumbs
- 1/2 cup crumbled feta cheese
- 2 scallions, finely diced
- juice of one lemon
- 1/2 teaspoon basil
- 1/2 teaspoon thyme
- 1/2 teaspoon salt
- 1/4 teaspoon black pepper

Artichokes:

- 4 large artichokes, tips of leaves trimmed, steamed or boiled until tender (about 40–50 minutes)

Preheat the oven to 350°.

In a small mixing bowl, combine all the ingredients except the artichokes. Stir until everything is well incorporated.

Pull the center leaves out of cooked artichokes. Scoop out the fuzzy layer in the middle. Remove 5 or 6 leaves at random spots around the artichoke to make a few spaces for filling.

Spoon the filling into the center you have hollowed out, creating a heaping mound of filling on top. Sprinkle the filling mixture in the spaces you've made around the artichoke and wherever else you can spread some of the leaves apart.

Place the filled artichokes in a baking dish and bake for 15 minutes, until the filling on top begins to brown slightly.

Serves 4.

How to prepare artichokes:

One of the most important rules is to cook fresh artichokes within 3 or 4 days of purchase. Raw artichokes don't stay fresh for long and can develop a hard-to-detect rotting mold deep in the center of the choke.

To prepare an artichoke, lay it on its side and cut off the stem even with the bottom of the plant. Cut 1 1/2 inches off the top leaves. Then use kitchen scissors to snip the thorny tip from each remaining exposed leaf. Rub half a lemon over the base and all cut sections of the artichoke to prevent discoloration. Soak the artichokes in lemon water until you are ready to cook them.

In a large stock pot, bring water, a tablespoon of lemon juice, and a tablespoon of olive oil to a boil. Add the artichokes, cover, and boil until tender. Small to medium artichokes (fist-sized) cook in about 25–35 minutes; large artichokes usually take 40–50 minutes.

Cooked artichokes may be refrigerated for up to 3–4 days for later consumption.

ORIENTAL NOODLES WITH TOFU AND PEANUT SAUCE

Dressing:

2 teaspoons chili paste

2 tablespoons grated fresh ginger

¹/₈ cup soy sauce

¹/₄ cup saki or white wine

¹/₄ cup peanut butter

¹/₂ teaspoon cayenne pepper (or to taste)

1 tablespoon sesame oil

2 cloves garlic, crushed

1 teaspoon cornstarch

6 tablespoons rice wine vinegar

Noodle Mix:

¹/₄ cup minced fresh cilantro leaves

¹/₃ cup roasted, unsalted peanuts

¹/₄ cup diced scallions

¹/₄ cup diced celery

1¹/₂ cups cut-up tofu, sliced in 1-inch cubes

1 16-ounce package Oriental noodles, boiled and drained

Combine the dressing ingredients in a small sauce pan over medium-high heat and bring to a boil. Stir constantly until the mixture is smooth and thickened.

In a large serving bowl, combine the cilantro, peanuts, scallions, celery, tofu, and cooked noodles. Pour the hot dressing over the noodles and toss well. Serve immediately.

Keeps well in the refrigerator for up to 2 days. Reheat in a skillet over medium-high heat, tossing for about 3 minutes until hot.

Serves 4.

Chinese and Japanese immigrants created significant communities in the Canadian Rockies during the construction of the Canadian rail system. Recently, Asian restaurants, from Japanese sushi bars to contemporary Chinese and Korean eateries, have gained new popularity in the Rocky Mountain West. The resurgence of their cultures through their cuisines is a positive trend that I have brought into my own kitchen.

STEAMED CARROTS AND ZUCCHINI WITH CHIPOTLE CHILI BUTTER

3 cups peeled, sliced carrots

3 cups sliced tiny, unpeeled zucchini

5 tablespoons butter

1 clove garlic, crushed

4 tablespoons finely minced onion

2 tablespoons puréed canned chipotle chilies in adobo sauce (or to taste)

¼ teaspoon black pepper

fresh parsley for garnish

In a large steamer basket, steam the carrots and zucchini for 3–5 minutes, until they are just beginning to get tender (they should still be quite crisp). Transfer them to a serving bowl.

Melt the butter in a small saucepan over medium heat. Add the garlic, onion, chilies, and pepper. Cook until the minced onions begin to sizzle—about 3 minutes.

Pour the butter sauce over the vegetables and toss. Garnish with fresh parsley and serve immediately.

Serves 4–6.

Gardening in the Rocky Mountain region has its set of unique challenges. While we may not have the same varieties of predatory bugs and molds as other areas, gardeners here deal with a shorter growing season and cold nights.

Many companies specializing in seeds for this region have done a terrific job. They have bred varieties that will ripen extra fast to try to beat that early fall frost, and at the same time will be hearty enough to survive the surprise frosts at the beginning of the season. The final results, regardless of how they are achieved, are worth it. A gardener can easily feel like every mouthful of garden produce is precious and deserving of extra care in the kitchen. This recipe is simple in a way that lets a gardener's skill shine.

CORN AND PEPPER CAKES

2 cups corn—frozen or cut fresh from the cob

½ cup finely diced red bell pepper

½ cup finely diced green bell pepper

2 cups mashed potatoes, cooled

2 scallions, finely chopped

⅛ cup cornmeal

⅛ cup flour

¾ teaspoon salt

¼ teaspoon freshly ground black pepper

4 egg whites

¼ cup nonfat or lowfat buttermilk

non-stick cooking spray

In a large mixing bowl, combine the vegetables, cornmeal, flour, salt, and pepper. Use a large mixing spoon to mix the ingredients well and remove any lumps.

In a separate bowl, whisk the egg whites until frothy. Add the buttermilk and mix. Fold the liquids into the corn mixture, stirring well.

Coat your hands with non-stick cooking spray and form the mixture into 8 or 10 small patties.

Coat a large skillet with additional non-stick spray and heat on a medium-high burner. Cook the patties until golden brown. If you like them extra crispy, turn the heat down to medium-low and cook longer, until the surface dries out. Then finish with higher heat for a couple of minutes.

Serve with fish, poultry, meat, or salad. For a vegetarian meal, cover with sautéed green chilies, onions, garlic, and black beans.

Makes approximately 8–10 cakes.

This recipe is a leftover concoction—a great way to combine lots of vegetables with binders like leftover potatoes or bread crumbs into pancakes or patties. Other similar combinations can include carrots, celery, broccoli, sweet potatoes, squash, and green beans. Substitute your favorite garden leftovers and blanch them to make your own version of this recipe.

WARM BALSAMIC FRIJOLE SALAD

2 cups dry pinto beans, cleaned and sorted

$^3/_4$ teaspoons salt

4 tablespoons extra virgin olive oil

$^1/_2$ cup finely diced red onion

2 cloves garlic, crushed

$^1/_2$ teaspoon dried thyme or 1 teaspoon fresh thyme

$^3/_4$ teaspoon salt

$^1/_4$ teaspoon freshly ground black pepper

$^1/_4$–$^1/_2$ teaspoon crushed red pepper flakes

1 red bell pepper, cleaned, seeded, and sliced into strips

$^1/_4$ cup balsamic vinegar

Pour the beans into a large stockpot and add water to at least 3 inches above the level of the beans. Add $^3/_4$ teaspoon salt. Bring the beans to a boil over medium-high heat. Skim the foam from the top of the liquid. Turn the heat down to medium-low and let the beans simmer for 2–3 hours, until they are just tender. All beans cook at a different rate, depending on their moisture content; check the beans after $1^1/_2$ hours to be sure they aren't cooking faster than usual. (To speed up the cooking time, presoak the beans in water overnight before cooking, then cook for approximately $1^1/_2$–$2^1/_2$ hours.)

Drain the cooked beans well, saving 1 cup of the cooking liquid.

Heat the olive oil in a sauté pan over medium heat. Cook the onion and garlic for just 1 or 2 minutes, until they begin to give off their distinct aroma. Add the cooked, drained beans and the remaining ingredients and combine well, removing from the heat after another minute. Serve warm.

May be prepared a day ahead and tossed in hot pan until warm just before serving.

Serves 4–6.

A jar of dried pinto beans may not seem like such a precious gift—except when it comes from Dove Creek, Colorado, the highly acclaimed pinto bean capital of the nation. A little town on Highway 666 near the southwestern Colorado-Utah border, Dove Creek has just the right soil for growing the most flavorful pinto beans. A friend of mine who visits family in New Mexico makes it a priority to stop there on his way back home to Montana. Various growers and markets in the Dove Creek area sell 20-pound bags for around $20.

WILD MUSHROOM AND WALNUT BREAD PUDDING WITH JARLSBERG

2 tablespoons butter

1 clove garlic, crushed

1/4 cup diced onion

3 cups sliced mushrooms—porcini, crimini, portabella, or morel

5 cups dense white or sourdough bread, sliced into 1-inch cubes

2 cups half-and-half

4 eggs

2 1/2 cups grated Jarlsberg cheese

1/2 cup whole walnuts

1 teaspoon dry mustard

1/2 teaspoon thyme

1/8 teaspoon freshly grated nutmeg

1/8 teaspoon cayenne pepper

1/4 teaspoon black pepper

1/2 teaspoon salt

Preheat the oven to 350°. Grease a 9 x 13-inch baking dish.

In a large mixing bowl, combine all the ingredients, stirring well to distribute the flavors.

Pour the mixture into the baking dish. Bake for 50 minutes or until set and golden.

Serves 6.

The hunt for edible wild mushrooms is a Rocky Mountain outdoor sport with its own loyal following. The moist, rich soil of Rocky Mountain forests holds great promise for hobby mycologists. However, this is not a hobby to be taken lightly. Poisonous mushrooms are often difficult to differentiate from edible mushrooms. Even the most detailed guidebooks can't replace learning to correctly identify mushrooms from someone who is very familiar with their characteristics. Never consume a wild mushroom without consulting a practiced forager as well as a carefully detailed guidebook.

NUTMEG SPÄTZLE

3¼ cups unbleached white flour

¾ teaspoon salt

¼ teaspoon freshly grated nutmeg

1 cup water

3 eggs, lightly beaten

Using an electric mixer, combine the flour, salt, and nutmeg. Add the water and beat well until smooth and thick. Add the eggs one at a time, beating after each addition until the dough is smooth and bubbly; it will still be tough.

Let the dough rest for 30 minutes.

Bring a large pot of water to a boil. Holding the dough bowl in one hand and a knife in the other, slice off slivers of dough—each no bigger than a teaspoonful in volume—into the boiling water. Another method is to press a third of the dough at a time through a colander into the boiling water, using the back of a wooden spoon. Don't crowd the dumplings in the pot; boil them in several batches. When the spätzle rise to the top after about 5 minutes, lift them out of the water with a slotted spoon.

Drain with cold water to prevent sticking and layer in a waiting dish, dotting each layer with butter. Reheat in warm oven before serving.

Serves 8–10.

I enjoy spätzle with wild game and stewed meat recipes and find they take well to just about any dressing-up. The chewy, firm texture of these German dumplings makes a variety of additions to the basic recipe possible. Try adding chopped nuts, bits of dried fruit, diced dried mushrooms, or fresh herbs to the dough. Also try boiling the spätzle in homemade chicken or beef broth for a simple and comforting winter soup.

SPICED RED RISOTTO

2 teaspoons extra virgin olive oil

⅓ cup finely diced red onion

1 clove garlic, crushed

½ cup uncooked Arborio rice

1 cup chicken stock

¼ cup port wine

2 cups beet juice

½ teaspoon paprika

¼ teaspoon cinnamon

⅛ teaspoon cloves

½ teaspoon cumin

¼ teaspoon salt

1 tablespoon butter

⅓ cup freshly grated Parmesan cheese

cilantro leaves and extra Parmesan cheese for garnish

Heat the olive oil in a medium-sized saucepan over medium-high heat. Add the onion and sauté for 10 minutes, until translucent. Add the garlic and raw rice and stir well to coat the rice with oil.

Add the chicken stock to the rice mixture. Stir and cook until the rice has nearly absorbed all the liquid. Next add the port wine; simmer again until the liquid is nearly absorbed.

Lower the heat and add ½ cup of beet juice, simmering until the liquid is almost absorbed. Repeat this process 2 more times, adding another ½ cup of beet juice each time. Along with the fourth and final ½ cup of beet juice, add the paprika, cinnamon, cloves, cumin, and salt. Simmer until most of the liquid on the surface is gone, then stir in the butter and Parmesan cheese.

Serve immediately, garnished with cilantro leaves and more grated Parmesan.

Serves 4.

The hallmarks of a good menu are a variety of bright colors, some contrasting textures, and many layers of flavor. Try the one below or combinations of your own, with a similar experimental flair in mind.

Suggested Menu:

- **Sea Bass in Cashew Crust with Gingered Apricot Sauce (page 108)**
- **Spiced Red Risotto**
- **Feta- and Lemon-Crumb Stuffed Artichokes (page 61)**
- **Walnut, Garlic, and Sun-dried Tomato Foccacia (page 159)**

Low
Fat

DRIED APPLE AND WALNUT QUINOA

  1 teaspoon light oil
¼ cup finely diced yellow onion
  1 teaspoon grated fresh ginger root
  2 cups vegetable stock or water
¼ teaspoon ground coriander
¼ teaspoon cinnamon
½ teaspoon salt
  1 cup quinoa
½ cup diced dried apples
¼ cup broken walnut pieces

In a medium-sized saucepan, sauté the onion in the oil over medium-high heat.

Add the ginger, stock, spices, salt, and quinoa. Stir and bring to a boil. Cover, reduce the heat to low, and simmer for 15 minutes.

Remove from the heat and stir in the apples and walnuts. Serve immediately.

Serves 4.

The first time I tasted the slightly bitter, nutty grain called quinoa (pronounced KEEN-wah), I was at a friend's wedding in an adobe home overlooking Santa Fe, New Mexico. This tiny, millet-sized grain is extremely high in protein, and is especially popular with restaurant chefs in the southern Rocky Mountain states of Colorado and New Mexico. Originally grown in South America, quinoa has been found in Incan ruins; it was apparently an important part of the Incan diet. Quinoa lends an unusual flavor to common dishes. Look for quinoa in natural food stores. Most often found in its white form, it is sometimes available in black, purple, and red.

GREEN CHILI PENNE PASTA WITH CILANTRO AND PINE NUTS

2 teaspoons olive oil
¼ cup diced yellow onion
3 cloves garlic, crushed
½ cup diced red bell pepper
½ cup white wine
7-ounce can diced green chilies
2 tablespoons minced fresh cilantro
½ teaspoon ground cumin
½ teaspoon salt
⅛ teaspoon cayenne pepper
¼ cup pine nuts

½ pound dry penne pasta, cooked al dente

cilantro leaves for garnish

Heat the oil in a large sauté pan over medium-high heat. Add the onion, garlic, bell pepper, and wine. Sauté until the vegetables start to soften, about 3 minutes.

Add the remaining ingredients and toss until the pasta is heated through.

Serve immediately with a few cilantro leaves as garnish.

Serves 4.

While cilantro often identifies a dish as Asian or Hispanic, this fresh leaf snipped from the coriander plant has become an herb associated with Rocky Mountain flavor, as well. Sometimes called Chinese parsley, cilantro has a vaguely anisey flavor that is quite different from the sweet essence of the coriander's seed, which is ground and used in everything from gingerbread to curry. Cilantro adds a distinct taste to any dish, a taste which some diners don't like.

Cilantro is used liberally in restaurants throughout the Rockies. I usually have no trouble finding a fresh bunch next to the parsley in most grocery stores. Cilantro perishes quickly, so it's best to keep the bundles root-end down in a jar of water. Cover the jar with a plastic bag and keep it in the refrigerator. When stored properly, the herb will last about a week.

AU GRATIN POTATOES WITH HORSERADISH

2 tablespoons butter

1 yellow onion, sliced in thin rounds

1 clove garlic, crushed

1 stalk celery, finely diced

2 tablespoons flour

⅛ teaspoon nutmeg

½ teaspoon salt

¼ teaspoon pepper

2 cups lowfat (2%) milk

½ cup grated Swiss cheese

4 tablespoons prepared horseradish

5 large potatoes, peeled and sliced in thin rounds

non-stick cooking spray

Preheat the oven to 400°. Lightly spray a baking dish with non-stick spray.

Melt the butter in a saucepan over medium heat. Add the onions, garlic, and celery. Cook for 5 minutes, stirring, until the vegetables soften.

Add the flour, nutmeg, salt, and pepper to the pan, stirring to dissolve. Slowly add the milk, cheese, and horseradish, whisking until the sauce is thickened and smooth.

Lay the potatoes in the baking dish. Pour the sauce over the top.

Bake for 50 minutes, until the potatoes are tender and a crust forms on top.

Serves 6.

Tuber roots like potatoes and pungent horseradish are common ingredients in the traditional cooking of cultures all over the world. In the Rocky Mountains, these roots were staples for Native American tribes, such as the Crow, Mandan, and Bannock, each developing its own culinary specialties.

SWEET POTATO HASH BROWNS
WITH JALAPEÑO AND RED ONION

6 cups washed, diced sweet potatoes—
  cut into 1-inch cubes with the skin left on

3 tablespoons butter

½ cup coarsely chopped red onion

1–3 jalapeños, diced—leave the seeds in for
  a hotter taste

½ teaspoon salt

ground black pepper to taste

Add the sweet potato cubes to a medium-sized saucepan of boiling, salted water. Boil until just tender, about 10 minutes. Drain in a colander.

Melt the butter in large non-stick fry pan over medium-high heat. Add the onion and jalapeños. Sauté for about 3 minutes, then add the potatoes, salt, and pepper. Mix well, lower the heat to medium, and cover pan. Cook until browned.

Serves 6.

By no means a complete listing of the chilies of the world, this short chili glossary may come in handy when you are faced with several varieties in the produce section of a grocery store.

Anaheim—pale green and about 6 inches long. The mildest cousin of the New Mexican green chili. Cans of mild green chilies are usually anaheims.

Ancho (also called Poblano or Pasilla)—dark green or red, 4–5 inches long, and 3–4 inches around. Medium to hot in strength, the ancho is always cooked or roasted.

Cayenne—bright red, thin, and tiny: ½-inch around. The cayenne's flavor is very hot and sweet. The cayenne is most often used in its dried, ground form.

Habañero—green, orange, or yellow and lantern-shaped. The hottest chili available in North American stores.

Jalapeño—light to dark green, or sometimes red, and about 1–3 inches long. The jalapeño is fairly hot, but especially good in flavor. When dried and smoked, jalapeños are called Chipotle chilies.

New Mexican Green—light to medium green and 4–6 inches long. The New Mexican green chili has a sweet earthy flavor and varies from medium to very hot in strength.

New Mexican Red—deep red. This is the ripened version of the New Mexican green chili. The New Mexican red chili is sweeter than the green version and often milder, but is still fiery.

GREEN CHILI GNOCCHI

6 large potatoes, baked in their skins until soft

2 cups unbleached white flour

¼ cup finely ground corn flour

¾ teaspoon salt

1 7-ounce can mild or hot green chilies, diced, or 4 diced jalapeños

freshly grated Parmesan

fresh cilantro leaves

Peel the potatoes and mash them coarsely with a fork or a potato masher. In a large mixing bowl, combine the potatoes, white flour, corn flour, salt, and green chilies. Mix well with a wooden spoon or your hands until the ingredients are well combined and the dough forms a ball.

Divide the dough into 4 workable pieces. Roll each piece on a floured surface with your hands, making a rope that is ½ inch in diameter. Cut each rope into 1-inch pieces. Spread the pieces out on a floured baking sheet or countertop to dry.

Bring a large stock pot of salted water to a boil.

Drop a handful of shaped dough into the boiling water to cook. When they begin to float, remove the gnocchi with a slotted spoon. Repeat with the next handful.

Place the gnocchi in a buttered baking dish and serve with tomato or béchamel sauce. Or, just cover them in onions and more green chilies sautéed in butter and garlic. Sprinkle with freshly grated Parmesan and cilantro leaves.

Serves 6–8.

While I don't make my green chili gnocchi in quite the same way as they do at the Old Santa Fe Trail Books and Coffeehouse, this recipe was born out of a visit to that quirky combination of classic bookstore and gourmet café. "Coffeehouse" is a deceptive description of this establishment, which is housed in an old Victorian home. Folks in the kitchen at the Old Santa Fe Trail Books and Coffeehouse have a bent toward preparing unpretentious food, with a flair for imaginative twists that I admire.

Gnocchi is a classic Italian potato dumpling side dish. Some people roll their gnocchi against the tine of a fork to leave a lined indentation in each dumpling. The cooks at the Old Santa Fe Trail Books and Coffeehouse don't worry much about the design of their dumplings. Still, their simple-looking gnocchi, dressed in just a little butter and cheese, are delightful.

CILANTRO PESTO

   2 cups cilantro leaves, firmly packed
$^3/_4$ cup Italian parsley leaves, firmly packed
$^1/_4$ cup pine nuts
   3 cloves garlic, crushed
$^3/_4$ cup freshly grated Parmesan cheese
$^1/_4$ teaspoon black pepper
$^1/_2$ teaspoon salt
$^1/_2$ teaspoon ground cumin
$^1/_4$ teaspoon red pepper flakes
$^1/_3$ cup extra virgin olive oil

Combine all the ingredients in a blender or food processor. Blend until the mixture has the consistency of paste, turning the blender or processor off twice during processing to scrape down the sides.

Toss the pesto in desired amounts with just-boiled pasta or black beans, or use in other recipes that call for pesto.

A variation on traditional pesto that is made with fresh basil, this version has unique Rocky Mountain appeal. Another version might substitute raw sunflower seeds for the pine nuts. The milder, nutty flavor of the sunflower seeds nicely balances the more pungent taste of the cilantro.

CHILI-ORANGE OIL

2¹/₂ cups canola oil

¹/₃ cup sesame oil

¹/₃ cup crushed hot pepper flakes

4 tablespoons Chinese salted black beans

zest of 2 oranges (wash the oranges first in soapy water)

3 cloves garlic, crushed

Combine all the ingredients in a medium saucepan over medium-low heat. Heat until the hot pepper flakes begin to bubble lightly. Remove from the heat, stir well, and let cool.

Pour the oil into a glass jar or sealable container and store in a dark, cool cupboard. Keeps well for up to 9 months.

Oils like this make great holiday gifts. Pour them into beautiful glass jars decorated with ribbon or raffia. Chili-Orange Oil is wonderful in stir-fry recipes, especially when combined with mild-flavored vegetables and meats.

Lamb, Pork, Wild Game, and Beef

Curried Lamb Stew with Chick Peas and Apricots

Denver Lamb in Ethiopian We't Marinade

Beer-Braised Root Vegetables and Pork Ribs

Roasted Pork Tenderloin with Olives and Artichokes

Mu Shu Pork

Sirloin Tip Roast in Chili-Ale Sauce

Coffee-Sage Roasted Elk

Cabernet-Cherry Grilled Elk Flank with Red Onion Marmalade

Mushroom Pasties with Burgundy Sauce

German Short Ribs with Juniper and Caraway

Venison with Fiery Huckleberry-Wine Sauce

Venison Schnitzel with Red Cabbage and Apples

Gorgonzola- and Walnut-Stuffed Beef Tenderloin with
Sun-dried Tomato Relish

Wild Herb Meat rub

CURRIED LAMB STEW WITH CHICK PEAS AND APRICOTS

1½ pounds lamb stew meat, trimmed of fat and cut into 1-inch chunks
1 tablespoon olive oil
3 cloves garlic, crushed
½ cup diced red onion
½ cup diced celery
½ cup diced carrot
1 tablespoon grated fresh ginger root
1 tablespoon hot curry powder
¼ teaspoon black pepper
¾ teaspoon salt
1½ cups apple cider

1 cup water
1 cup chicken broth
2 tablespoons fresh lime juice
6 tablespoons mango chutney
1 15-ounce can chick peas with their liquid
½ cup diced dried apricots

Heat the olive oil in a large Dutch oven or heavy pot over medium-high heat. Brown the lamb chunks.

Add the garlic and vegetables and sauté for 8 minutes, until the vegetables begin to soften.

Stir in the ginger, curry powder, pepper, salt, apple cider, water, chicken broth, and lime juice. Cover, lower the heat, and let simmer for 1 hour.

Add the chutney, chick peas, and apricots to the stew, stir, and simmer uncovered for another 15 minutes. Check the seasonings, adding more curry, salt, and pepper if desired.

Serves 4–6.

Even though my grandma, Betty Woodcock Willits, grew up on a ranch that raised sheep in the Shonkin Mountain area near Highwood, Montana, beef was the most popular red meat at family dinners. Maybe the fact that many sheep ranchers end up eating the oldest and toughest mutton at their own tables makes beef that much more appealing to them.

Lamb is the focus of a sizable ranching business in the Rocky Mountain region, so I'm often surprised at the number of restaurants in the area that don't even have it on their menus. Many people avoid lamb after having had just one serving of an old, tough cut of mutton. But the young, carefully bred lamb you can purchase at your local store is mild and lean. For those who enjoy distinctly flavored food, try lamb in strongly spiced dishes that include curry, red chili pepper, and herbs like rosemary and cilantro.

DENVER LAMB IN ETHIOPIAN WE'T MARINADE

1 cup finely minced red onions

1¼ cup water (more if needed)

¼ cup butter

½ cup berbere (a red pepper combination of spices)

½ cup red wine

1 pound lamb loin, trimmed of fat and cubed

¼ teaspoon cardamom

1 tablespoon grated fresh ginger root

¼ teaspoon cumin

2 cloves garlic, crushed

¼ teaspoon freshly ground black pepper

⅛ teaspoon ground cloves

1 jalapeño pepper, seeded and finely minced

½ teaspoon salt

Pour ¼ cup of water into a large stock pot over low heat. Cook the onions in the water for 30–45 minutes. Stir frequently to make sure they don't stick or brown. Add additional water if necessary.

Add the butter, berbere seasoning, and wine. Stir and keep simmering on low .

Meanwhile, spray a separate pan with a small amount of cooking spray, or melt a tablespoon of butter in it. Brown the lamb meat in this pan.

Add the meat and the remaining ingredients to the onion mixture. Let simmer for 15–20 minutes more.

Serve with Ethiopian injera bread if available or pita bread, rice, or coarsely mashed potatoes, and plain yogurt or cottage cheese to calm your tongue.

Serves 4.

Colorado ranchers are known for raising lambs that produce a meat far superior to the often touted Australian lamb. Restaurant chefs across the country are vocal about their preference for Rocky Mountain lamb meat, whether it is from New Mexico, Utah, Wyoming, Idaho, Montana, or Colorado.

An Ethiopian recipe may seem out of place in a Rocky Mountain gourmet cookbook, but the popularity of this exotic and carefully flavored African cuisine is evident in at least one busy restaurant, Denver's The Ethiopian. Pairing Colorado lamb with Ethiopian cooking techniques is a natural marriage, since natives of Ethiopia frequently serve lamb and honor the tender, pungent meat with rare and precious herbs and spices like bishop's weed, fenugreek, turmeric, cardamom, and coriander.

BEER-BRAISED ROOT VEGETABLES WITH PORK RIBS

1 tablespoon vegetable oil
2 pounds boneless pork short ribs
2 teaspoons paprika
½ teaspoon salt
¼ teaspoon black pepper
2 carrots, peeled and cut into 3-inch slices
2 parsnips, peeled and cut into 3-inch slices
2 turnips, peeled and cut into 3-inch slices
2 white potatoes, peeled and cut into 3-inch slices

1 large yellow onion, chopped coarsely
2 cloves garlic, crushed
1 teaspoon thyme
1 teaspoon rosemary leaves
¼ teaspoon sage
2 cups flat beer
3 cups beef stock
1 bay leaf
10 ounces egg noodles, cooked and drained

Preheat the oven to 400°.

In a large Dutch oven or roasting pan over medium-high heat, brown the short ribs in the vegetable oil. Turn the ribs as they cook so they are browned on all sides.

Add all the remaining ingredients except the egg noodles to the pot. Stir to combine, remove from the heat, and cover.

Place the pot in the oven and bake until the ribs are tender, about 1½ hours. Add additional salt and pepper to taste.

Serve over noodles.

Serves 4–6.

Beer-Braised Root Vegetables with Pork Ribs makes a perfect, earthy winter meal. Preparing it will warm up a chilled kitchen and fill the house with the strong meat and vegetable scents that can only come from cooking something slowly.

Quick meals are a godsend on a hurried weekday evening, but for me, weekends are about slow-cooked meals. The food has time to grow into its richest flavor during a long, slow cook. If you plan ahead and drop any of my slow-cooking recipes into a crock pot, you'll have the slow-cooked taste and a relaxed hour before dinner, too.

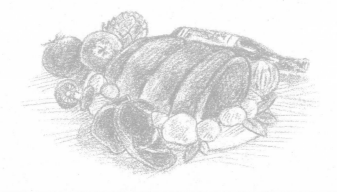

ROASTED PORK TENDERLOIN WITH OLIVES AND ARTICHOKES

2 cloves garlic, crushed

juice of 1 lemon (reserve 1 tablespoon for the artichoke sauce)

1 teaspoon lemon zest

3 tablespoons honey

2 tablespoons Dijon-style mustard

2 pounds pork tenderloins, trimmed of fat

2 tablespoons extra virgin olive oil

1/2 cup diced red onion

1/2 teaspoon crushed rosemary

1/4 teaspoon black pepper

1/4 teaspoon salt

1/2 cup diced black olives

1/2 cup diced pimento-stuffed green olives

2 7-ounce jars marinated artichoke hearts with juice

1/2 cup dry white wine

1 teaspoon cornstarch dissolved in the white wine

Preheat the oven to 375°.

In a small bowl, combine 1 of the cloves of crushed garlic, the bulk of the lemon juice, the zest, the honey, and the mustard, mixing to combine well. Rub this mixture over the pork tenderloins.

Roast the pork in a baking pan for 15–20 minutes, depending upon desired level of doneness. Try to leave the pork as pink as you can for maximum tenderness.

While the pork is roasting, heat the olive oil in a skillet over medium-high heat. Sauté the onion and the other clove of garlic in the oil for 5 minutes. Add the remaining tablespoon of lemon juice along with the rosemary, black pepper, salt, olives, and artichokes with their marinade. Dissolve the cornstarch in the white wine and add this mixture to the pan too. Continue to stir and simmer for 10 minutes, until the sauce is slightly thickened.

When the pork is done, remove it from the oven and slice it against the grain into medallions. Serve topped with artichoke sauce over rice or pasta.

Serves 4–6.

Since pork marries well with sweet flavors, roll a tenderloin in just about any preserve, spice it up with complementary herbs, and roast it quickly. I've enjoyed pork tenderloin cooked in everything from apricot preserves with fresh ginger to Louisiana hot sauce mixed with currant jelly.

Other cooking ideas include rolling a tenderloin in sesame seeds and grated lemon rind, roasting it until it's crisp, and slicing it on a baguette roll with Chinese mustard and shredded cabbage. Or, try slicing the tenderloins down the center and stuffing them with a mixture of chopped spinach, feta cheese, and bread crumbs before roasting them; then serve them with good quality olive oil infused with fresh garlic and red peppers.

Try to resist the urge to cook all the pink out of the pork tenderloin. It's perfectly safe at 160° as tested with a meat thermometer, and far superior in texture and flavor to the more well-done pork roasts.

MU SHU PORK

20 Mu Shu Wrappers, (see recipe page 158)

3 tablespoons soy sauce

3 tablespoons dry sherry

2 teaspoons sesame oil

2 teaspoons cornstarch

2 teaspoons granulated sugar

3/4 pound pork tenderloin, cut into matchstick-sized pieces

1 tablespoon vegetable oil

1 clove garlic, crushed

1 teaspoon grated fresh ginger root

5 tree ear mushrooms, thinly sliced, soaked in hot water for 30 minutes, and drained

6 scallions, cut into 2-inch lengths then shredded lengthwise

3/4 cup bamboo shoots, cut like matchsticks

2 carrots, shredded into strips with a vegetable peeler

3 cups shredded iceberg lettuce

5 eggs, scrambled

hoisin sauce

Prepare the Mu Shu Wrappers ahead of time.

In a bowl, combine the soy sauce, sherry, sesame oil, cornstarch, sugar, and cut-up pork. Mix well.

Heat the vegetable oil in a wok. Add the pork mixture, garlic, and ginger. Fry for about 5 minutes, stirring constantly. Add the tree ears and stir for another minute. Add half the scallions and all the bamboo shoots, carrots, and lettuce. Stir-fry for about 2 more minutes, until the lettuce wilts. Stir in the eggs and pour the entire contents of the wok into a serving dish.

Serve immediately: Arrange the prepared pancakes, the hoisin sauce, and the remaining shredded green onion on the table. Have the diners spread sauce on a pancake, fill it with pork filling, top it with shredded green onion, fold it, and eat it with their hands.

Serves 4.

Mu Shu Pork was popular with the Chinese miners and railroad laborers who settled in the Rocky Mountains in the 19th century. Obviously, a creative cook can play with the recipe, making any number of substitutions for a different flair. I especially enjoy sliced pheasant breast in place of pork in this recipe.

Low Fat

SIRLOIN TIP ROAST IN CHILI-ALE SAUCE

2–2½ pound sirloin tip roast,
    well trimmed of fat

1 medium-sized yellow onion,
    coarsely chopped

salt and freshly ground black pepper to taste

½ teaspoon dried thyme leaves

1 cup flat ale-style beer

⅓ cup bottled chili sauce

3 cloves garlic, crushed

3 tablespoons flour

½ cup water

Preheat the oven to 350°.

Lay the roast in the center of a deep-sided baking or roasting pan. Sprinkle the chopped onion, salt, and pepper over the meat.

In a small bowl, mix together the thyme, ale, chili sauce, and garlic. Pour this mixture over the roast. Cover the pan.

Roast for about 1½ hours, until the meat is brown and tender. At least 2 or 3 times during roasting, baste the meat with the sauce in the pan.

Remove the meat to a carving board.

Pour the basting liquid into a saucepan and place on the stove over medium heat. Combine the flour and water. Whisk this mixture into the sauce until it bubbles, about 3–5 minutes.

Slice the meat and serve with the sauce over noodles.

Serves 4–6.

A full-bodied bottle or can of locally brewed beer has always been easy to find in the Rockies. Many Rocky Mountain breweries started making beer back in the late 1800s. With the surge in popularity of microbrewed beer, new breweries have sprouted up throughout the region. My favorite, by far, is the Great Northern Brewing Company in Whitefish, Montana. They brew a wild huckleberry beer I adore, with its mild hint of natural wild berry flavor. Some other excellent Rocky Mountain breweries include the New Belgium Brewery in Fort Collins, Colorado; Wynkoop Brewing Company in Denver, Colorado; Red Rock Brewing in Salt Lake City, Utah; Snake River Brewing Company in Jackson, Wyoming; and Tablerock Brewery in Boise, Idaho.

COFFEE-SAGE ROASTED ELK

3–4 pound elk roast
1 large onion, sliced
3 cloves garlic, slivered
$1/4$ cup red wine
4 tablespoons balsamic vinegar
2 cups coffee
5 strips smoked bacon
salt and pepper to taste
$1/2$ teaspoon sage
$1/4$ teaspoon thyme
$1/4$ teaspoon cayenne pepper

1 cup water
1 tablespoon cornstarch

Cut slits into the roast and stuff with slices of onion and garlic. Place the roast in a sealable container.

Mix together the wine, 2 tablespoons of the balsamic vinegar, and 1 cup of the coffee. Pour this mixture over the roast. Marinate in the refrigerator overnight, turning several times.

Preheat the oven to 350°.

On the stove over medium-high heat, brown 1 piece of bacon in a heavy Dutch oven or roasting pan. Remove the roast from its marinade (reserve the liquid) and brown it in the pan, turning to sear both sides.

Lay the 4 other pieces of bacon over the roast in the pan. Sprinkle with salt and pepper.

Add the sage, thyme, cayenne, extra cup of coffee, remaining 2 tablespoons of balsamic vinegar, and water to the marinade in the sealable container. Mix and pour over the roast.

Cover the meat and roast it for $1^1/2$–2 hours, until tender.

Remove the meat to a cutting board. Pour the pan drippings into a saucepan, whisk in the cornstarch, and stir over medium heat until thickened.

Serve the roast sliced with potatoes, mashed or fried, and gravy.

Serves 6–8.

Whether you use ranch-raised beef sirloin or a cut of wild game, a coffee-marinated roast is about as authentic as you can get in the world of cowboy cooking. I admit the taste is a bit unusual, but the bitterness of the coffee mellows to a cappucino-style smoothness when slow-cooked with red meat.

I've dressed up this simple method of cooking, adding the sweet taste of balsamic vinegar and the regional herb, sage. If you find the coffee taste pleasant but too strong, substitute water for the last cup of coffee in this recipe.

CABERNET-CHERRY GRILLED ELK FLANK WITH RED ONION MARMALADE

Marinade:

- 1 cinnamon stick
- 1 cup cabernet sauvignon
- 2 cloves garlic, crushed
- 3 tablespoons lemon juice
- 1 cup diced pitted cherries
- 1/2 teaspoon freshly ground black pepper
- 1/2 teaspoon salt
- 2 teaspoons cornstarch

- 2 –2 1/2 pounds elk or beef flank steak

Marmalade:

- 5 cups red onions, sliced into thin rings and separated
- 2 tablespoons olive oil
- 1/2 cup honey
- 1/3 cup red wine vinegar
- 2 tablespoons balsamic vinegar
- 1/4 cup golden raisins
- 1 tablespoon grated fresh ginger root
- 1/2 teaspoon dried thyme leaves
- 1/4 teaspoon cayenne pepper
- 1/2 teaspoon salt

In a shallow dish or a large resealable plastic bag, combine the marinade ingredients, except the cornstarch. Add the steak, coating it well. Marinate the steak in the refrigerator, covered or sealed in the bag, for at least 6 hours or overnight. Turn the meat or shake the bag several times during marination.

To prepare the marmalade, measure the olive oil into a skillet over medium-high heat. Sauté the onions in the oil, stirring occasionally, until tender—about 15 minutes.

Add the remaining marmalade ingredients to the skillet and cook, uncovered, for about 25 minutes. The marmalade can be prepared ahead and refrigerated for up to 3 days. Reheat before serving.

Prepare the grill. When the coals are ready, remove the steak from its marinade and put it on the grill. For medium-rare meat, cook for about 5 minutes on each side; for medium to well-done meat, cook each side 8–10 minutes.

To make a sauce, pour the marinade into a medium-sized saucepan. Whisk in the 2 teaspoons of cornstarch and bring to a low boil over medium heat. Stir until thickened and smooth.

Ladle cabernet sauce onto each dinner plate. Arrange slices of steak over the sauce and spoon red onion marmalade on top.

Serves 4–6.

Because game animals have fed on things other than the domestic grain we feed our ranch animals, their meat can have muddy, sour, or sagey flavors. I've found that both wine and beer can increase the palatability of game meats. Take care when cooking wild game: the lack of marbling or fat makes some game meats easy to overcook.

MUSHROOM PASTIES WITH BURGUNDY SAUCE

Pastry:

- 3 cups flour
- ³/₄ teaspoon salt
- ¹/₂ teaspoon dried thyme
- 1 cup vegetable shortening
- ¹/₂ cup very cold water

Filling:

- 4 tablespoons butter
- 1 pound mushrooms—a single variety or a combination of favorite types
- 1 clove garlic, crushed
- 2 large yellow onions, sliced in coarse chunks
- 1 tablespoon cornstarch
- ¹/₂ cup burgundy wine
- ¹/₂ teaspoon dried thyme
- ¹/₂ teaspoon dried rosemary
- ¹/₂ teaspoon dried parsley
- ¹/₄ teaspoon ground sage
- ³/₄ teaspoon salt
- ¹/₄ teaspoon freshly ground black pepper
- 1¹/₂ pounds beef loin tip, skirt, or flank steak, sliced into 2-inch cubes
- 5 medium-sized red potatoes, sliced into 2-inch cubes
- 3 large carrots, peeled and cubed

Sauce:

- 3 tablespoons butter
- 2 tablespoons flour
- 1 cup beef broth
- ¹/₂ cup burgundy wine
- ¹/₂ teaspoon salt
- ¹/₄ teaspoon black pepper
- ¹/₄ teaspoon rosemary

To make the pastry: Mix together the flour, salt, and thyme. Cut in the shortening with a pastry knife—or use a food processor—until the mixture resembles small pebbles. Add enough water to make a dough, stirring or processing until the mixture forms a ball. The dough should be slightly stickier than a traditional pie dough. Divide the dough into 6 equal pieces and roll each into an oblong round. Stack the pasties on a plate and cover them so they stay moist while you prepare the filling.

Preheat the oven to 375°. Grease a baking sheet.

Melt the butter for the filling in a skillet over medium-high heat. Add the mushrooms (whole), garlic, and onions. Sauté for 5 minutes.

Dissolve the cornstarch in the wine, and add this mixture to the skillet along with the herbs, salt, and pepper. Stir and cook until thickened and bubbling. Remove the skillet from the heat and allow to partially cool.

Stir the meat, potatoes, and carrots into the mushroom mixture.

Spoon this filling onto 1 side of each pastry round. Fold the pastry in half over the filling to form a half-moon shape. Crimp along the edges to seal. Place on the greased baking sheet.

Bake the pasties for 1 hour.

While the pasties bake, make the sauce. Melt the butter in a small saucepan and stir in the flour. Whisk in the beef broth, wine, salt, pepper, and rosemary. Stir until the sauce thickens and bubbles.

Keep the sauce hot until the pasties are done. Spoon some onto each plate and top with a hot pasty.

Serves 6.

The pasty, a simple meat and vegetable pie, was the traditional lunch for the Cornish miners who settled in large numbers near the mines in Colorado and Montana.

GERMAN SHORT RIBS WITH JUNIPER AND CARAWAY

1 tablespoon vegetable oil

3½ pounds boneless beef short ribs from the chuck, cut into 3-inch sections

2 large onions, chopped

4 cloves garlic, crushed

1 15-ounce can diced stewed tomatoes

5 tablespoons tomato paste

¼ teaspoon ground cloves

1 teaspoon caraway seeds

10 juniper berries

2 cups Gewürztraminer wine

1 14½-ounce can low-sodium beef broth

salt and pepper to taste

Heat the vegetable oil in a heavy pot over medium-high heat. Brown the short ribs on both sides in the oil.

Remove the short ribs to a plate and add the onions and garlic to the pan. Sauté for 4 minutes. Add the rest of the ingredients and stir to combine the flavors.

Return the ribs to the pan. Bring the liquid to a boil, then reduce the heat and simmer, covered, for 1 hour.

Remove the lid and simmer for another 45 minutes, until the ribs are very tender. Serve with Spätzle or noodles.

Serves 6.

While I consider the strong piney scent and flavor of juniper berries to be an especially Rocky Mountain flavor, the berries have been used in traditional German cooking for centuries. These low-growing evergreen shrubs are actually native to Europe.

The berries are known for being the principal flavoring in gin. They are extremely pungent; it rarely takes more than 15 of the tiny blue-black berries to inject their flavor into a dish. Most often used with other strongly flavored foods, they stand up well to peppery, vinegary, and salty flavors.

You can often find juniper berries in the bulk herb and spice sections of natural food stores. Or you can pick the berries directly from the bushes—just be sure they have not been treated with any chemicals.

Low
Fat

VENISON WITH FIERY HUCKLEBERRY-WINE SAUCE

1 tablespoon extra virgin olive oil

4 tablespoons finely minced red onion

1 cup fresh, frozen, or canned huckleberries

2½ cups red zinfandel wine

½ teaspoon red pepper flakes

1 tablespoon freshly squeezed lemon juice

2 teaspoons cornstarch

¼ teaspoon freshly ground black pepper

½ teaspoon salt

½ teaspoon thyme

4–6 venison steaks—or beef sirloin steaks

Heat the oil in a medium-sized saucepan over medium heat. Sauté the onion in the oil for 5 minutes. Whisk in the remaining ingredients (except the steaks) and bring to a boil. Lower the heat and simmer for 10 minutes, uncovered, until the sauce is smooth and thickened.

Grill or broil the steaks, as you would beef, according to taste. Serve with the sauce.

Serves 4–6.

Sweet-tart fruits can be successfully paired with spicy peppers in a way that does both flavors justice. Some people don't care for the taste of sweet sauces on their meats, such as fish fillets in a fresh berry sauce or sweet and sour pork recipes. Leaving out additional sugars in a fruit-based meat sauce can make it truly savory. The tart nuances of many fruits help temper the fire of peppers, so that one can sense the real pepper flavor instead of just the hot taste. I've played with various combinations: apricots with habañero chilies; blackberries with an immense amount of cracked pepper in a seafood crust; and applesauce with cinnamon and cayenne. The combination of huckleberries and red pepper flakes in this sauce is by far my favorite. If you're one who likes more sweet in your sauces, add some honey or brown sugar to this recipe.

VENISON SCHNITZEL WITH RED CABBAGE AND APPLES

1/4 cup flour

1/4 teaspoon paprika

1/4 teaspoon celery salt

1/4 teaspoon onion salt

2 eggs, beaten

1 cup fine dry bread crumbs

4 small center-cut boneless venison loins, sliced into 8 1/2-inch-thick cutlets—or use pork cutlets

8 tablespoons butter

2 cups water

1 piece smoked bacon

1 small head red cabbage, shredded

1 medium onion, diced

2 Granny Smith apples, diced with the peel left on

2 tablespoons brown sugar

1/8 teaspoon ground cloves

1 cup apple juice

5 tablespoons cider vinegar

1/2 teaspoon caraway seeds

Combine the flour, paprika, celery salt, and onion salt in a small bowl. Set it next to the bowl of beaten egg and a plate with the bread the crumbs on it. Dredge the cutlets first in the flour mixture, then in the egg, then in the bread crumbs.

Melt the butter in a non-stick skillet over medium-high heat. Brown the cutlets on both sides. Add the water and cover the pan. Lower the heat and simmer for about 40 minutes or until the meat is tender.

While the schnitzel is cooking, brown the bacon in a large pot over medium-high heat. Break the bacon into pieces and add the cabbage, onions, and apples. Stir and sauté for 5 minutes.

Add the remaining ingredients to the pot, stir well, and cover. Reduce the heat and simmer for 15 minutes.

Serve the cabbage-apple mixture as a bed for the venison schnitzel. Ladle gravy from the schnitzel pan over the top.

Serves 4.

Suggested Oktoberfest Menu:

- **Dried Mushroom Caviar with rye toasts (page 15)**
- **Fresh Vegetable Soup (page 26)**
- **Venison Schnitzel with Red Cabbage and Apples**
- **Root Vegetable Au Gratin with Nutmeg (page 55)**
- **Asparagus with Toasted Hazelnuts and Garlic (page 54)**
- **Bavarian Red Potato and Apple Salad (page 40)**
- **Cheddar Biscuits with Thyme and Sage (page 161)**
- **Ginger Oatmeal Cake (page 124)**

GORGONZOLA- AND WALNUT-STUFFED BEEF TENDERLOIN WITH SUN-DRIED TOMATO RELISH

Filling:

- ¼ cup crumbled Gorgonzola cheese
- ¼ cup coarsely sliced walnuts
- 1 teaspoon dried basil
- ¼ cup mayonnaise
- 1 clove garlic, crushed
- ¼ teaspoon black pepper

- 6 beef tenderloin fillets with pockets cut halfway through their centers

Relish:

- ¼ cup oil-packed sun-dried tomatoes, diced
- ¼ cup diced scallion
- ¼ cup diced celery
- ¼ cup diced red onion
- ¼ cup diced carrot
- 2 tablespoons balsamic vinegar
- 1 teaspoon dried basil
- ¼ teaspoon salt
- ¼ cup country-style mustard

Combine the filling ingredients, mixing well. Stuff about 2–3 tablespoons of filling into the cavity cut in the center of each fillet.

Broil or grill the tenderloin steaks according to taste.

Combine the relish ingredients in a small saucepan. Heat on a medium burner until just hot. The relish can be made ahead of time, refrigerated, and reheated.

Spoon the relish over the grilled tenderloin fillets and serve immediately.

Serves 6.

I gleaned this recipe idea from a special on the menu at the Gallatin Gateway Inn, 12 miles southwest of Bozeman, Montana, and just an hour from Yellowstone National Park. Built as a railroad hotel in the 1920s, the Spanish-style inn was designated a National Historic Landmark in 1980. Elegant, yet warmly comfortable, the inn houses one of Montana's most consistently superb restaurants. The current style of the restaurant's cuisine is very much contemporary Rocky Mountain gourmet, and includes recipes made with game.

Low Fat

WILD HERB MEAT RUB

½ teaspoon ground cinnamon

½ teaspoon coriander

½ teaspoon cumin

½ teaspoon black pepper

½ teaspoon thyme

1 tablespoon salt

1 teaspoon sugar

Combine all the ingredients and rub thoroughly over raw meat.

This rub is good with any fresh meat that you plan to roast, broil, or barbecue. Its peppery flavor is especially delicious with wild game. Most wild game will improve in flavor if you pepper it before cooking, and the other herbs in this rub will add an extra zing without overpowering the taste of the meat. Fresh cilantro leaves make a nice garnish for meat cooked with this rub.

Poultry and Wild Fowl

Parchment Chicken with Ginger and Hot Sesame Oil

Jerk-Style Grilled Pheasant

Pheasant Breasts in Apple-Sage Fricassee

Chipotle- and Thyme-Roasted Turkey Breast with Chipotle Aioli

Lemon-Sesame Roasted Chicken with Sesame Roasted Garlic Heads

Chili-Chocolate Chicken Satay with Peanut-Cucumber Relish

Orange Tea Duck

Quail with Fennel and Tarragon Cream

Braised Grouse Marsala

Three Pepper Penne with Chicken

Low Fat

PARCHMENT CHICKEN WITH GINGER AND HOT SESAME OIL

2 tablespoons grated fresh ginger root

3 teaspoons hot chili sesame oil

2 cloves garlic, crushed

2 scallions, diced

2 tablespoons lemon juice

2 tablespoons orange juice

1 tablespoon soy sauce

½ teaspoon salt

2 cups shredded cabbage

4 large sheets parchment paper, 12 x 15 inches

4 chicken breast halves, boneless and skinless

Preheat the oven to 400°.

In small bowl, whisk together the ginger, sesame oil, garlic, scallions, lemon juice, orange juice, soy sauce, and salt. Set this mixture aside.

Mound ¹/₂ cup of cabbage in the center of each of the 4 sheets of parchment. Lay a chicken breast on top of each mound of cabbage. Spoon about 2 tablespoons of the ginger mixture over each breast. Fold the pieces of parchment up around the chicken breasts, joining the edges above the meat; fold several times to seal. Lay the parchment packages in a shallow dish. Bake for 15 minutes.

Present the parchment packages at the table on individual serving plates. Slice them open before your guests' eyes for the striking release of steam from the parchment.

Serves 4.

The dramatic presentation of parchment-wrapped food is a simple way to create a special dish from average ingredients. Wrapping food in parchment for baking is actually a method of steaming. It's an effective way to hold flavors close in to the food, so the herbs and seasonings permeate the entire contents of the wrapping. Foil can be used with equal success, but without the pleasing visual effect of the delicate-looking parchment paper.

Parchment is obviously more environmentally friendly than foil packaging. Most cooking stores, as well as a growing number of grocers, carry parchment. Poultry and seafood are the best animal proteins to use with parchment. Vegetables also work well in parchment, alone or combined with proteins. I try to use several brightly colored ingredients, so they can be seen through the paper.

JERK-STYLE GRILLED PHEASANT

2 tablespoons vegetable oil

1 large onion, finely diced

4 whole scallions, chopped

4 cloves garlic, crushed

4 jalapeño peppers, seeded and minced

³/₄ teaspoon allspice

¹/₈ teaspoon cloves

³/₄ teaspoon thyme

¹/₄ teaspoon red pepper flakes

1 teaspoon salt

¹/₃ cup dark rum

3 tablespoons fresh lime juice

4 pheasant or chicken breasts and 4 hind legs with thigh and drum stick attached, skinned

Prepare the jerk seasoning the day before you plan to grill the poultry. Heat the oil in a skillet over medium heat. Add the onions, scallions, garlic, jalapeños, spices, and herbs, and sauté until the onions are soft. Stir in the salt, rum, and lime juice, and simmer until the liquid is cooked away. Cool.

Rub the jerk mixture over the pheasant pieces. Marinate at least 24 hours and up to 36 hours for the strongest flavor.

Prepare the barbecue grill with the addition of water-soaked hickory or mesquite chips scattered over the coals. Grill or broil the pheasant pieces for 8–12 minutes on each side, checking for doneness with a knife against the bone until no redness is left in the meat.

Serves 4.

Because this is a Rocky Mountain cookbook, some readers might assume this pheasant recipe involves making jerky, of the kind that mountain men gnawed on for high country meals. Actually, the style of cooking I'm using here has its origins in Jamaican culture. The jerk seasoning mixture is a combination of hot, sweet, and pungent herbs and spices. After the meat is marinated in the seasonings for days, it is roasted.

PHEASANT BREASTS IN APPLE-SAGE FRICASSEE

5 tablespoons all-purpose flour

1/4 teaspoon salt

1/4 teaspoon black pepper

1/4 teaspoon paprika

4 pheasant breast halves,
boneless and skinless—or substitute chicken

3 tablespoons olive oil

1/2 cup diced onion

1/2 cup diced celery

1/2 cup diced red bell pepper

1 clove garlic, crushed

1/2 cup calvados (brandy)

1/2 teaspoon sage

1 cup half-and-half

1 cup chicken or pheasant stock

2 Granny Smith apples, cored and
diced with the peel left on

In a small bowl, combine the flour, salt, pepper, and paprika. Dredge the pheasant breasts in this mixture.

Heat the olive oil in a non-stick skillet over medium-high heat. Brown the breasts on both sides, about 4 minutes a side. Remove from the skillet and set aside on a plate.

Add the onion, celery, red pepper, and garlic to the skillet and sauté, stirring frequently, for about 5 minutes or until the vegetables are soft. You may need to lower the heat to prevent the vegetables from browning.

Sprinkle 2 tablespoons of the flour mixture over the vegetables and stir for 1 minute to dissolve. Whisk the calvados, sage, half-and-half, and stock into the skillet. Stir until the mixture is smooth and beginning to thicken.

Put the pheasant breasts and apples into the skillet and simmer on low for 10 minutes, spooning the sauce over the meat a couple of times. Season with salt and pepper to taste. Serve over egg noodles or rice.

Serves 4.

For my tastes there is no finer fowl than pheasant—especially wild pheasant, but also the domestic bird popular in French and Chinese recipes. I learned from my mother to regard wild game as special, quality meat, rather than as something to use up from the freezer so you could move on to the domestic meat. When it comes time to cook with pheasant, I am so thankful for the bird's presence in my freezer. Many a pheasant hunter comes out of a season without a single taste. Far superior to chicken in my mind, with rich, fine-textured meat, pheasant deserves the best accompanying ingredients and most prized recipes.

CHIPOTLE- AND THYME-ROASTED TURKEY BREAST WITH CHIPOTLE AIOLI

Aioli:

3 cloves garlic, crushed

2 tablespoons puréed chipotle chilies in adobo sauce

4 tablespoons fresh lemon juice

$1/2$ teaspoon salt

1 teaspoon Dijon mustard

$3/4$ cup olive oil

Turkey:

3–4 pound turkey breast, boneless, with the skin left on

3 tablespoons pureed chipotle chilies in adobo sauce

2 cloves garlic, mashed with $1/2$ teaspoon of salt

1 teaspoon thyme

To prepare the aioli, purée the garlic, chipotle, lemon juice, salt, and mustard in a food processor or blender. With the machine running, pour the oil very slowly into the center of the mixture in a thin, steady stream. Continue blending until the aioli is thick and firm. Refrigerate until ready to use.

Preheat the oven to 350° for the turkey.

In a small bowl, combine the chipotle, garlic, and thyme from the second list of ingredients. Press your hand into the space between the turkey's skin and breast flesh to make a cavity. Rub the chipotle-thyme mixture into the cavity, spreading it over the breast.

Roast the turkey on a rack in the oven for 60–80 minutes, until the juices run clear when a knife is inserted into the side of the breast. Remove from the oven and let sit for 15 minutes before slicing. Slice and serve with chipotle aioli.

Serves 6.

This recipe allows you to offer a twist on traditional Thanksgiving fare without totally abandoning the expected courses and ingredients. Have a little fun with the following holiday menu.

Suggested Menu:

- Black Bean and Jalapeño Quesadillas (page 10)
- Southwestern Butternut Squash Soup (page 23)
- Chipotle and Thyme Roasted Turkey Breast with Chipotle Aioli
- Dried Apple and Walnut Quinoa (page 69)
- Stuffed Vegetables with Pine Nuts (page 59)
- Savory Chocolate and Red Chili Breadsticks (page 167)
- Spiced Native American Blue Corn Pudding (page 131)

LEMON-SESAME ROASTED CHICKEN WITH SESAME ROASTED GARLIC HEADS

grated zest of 1 lemon

1 clove garlic, crushed

3 tablespoons sesame oil

juice of one lemon

$^1/_2$ cup sherry

salt and pepper to taste

1 whole roasting chicken, rinsed well and patted dry

4 heads garlic

Preheat the oven to 350°.

In a small bowl, combine the lemon zest, the crushed clove of garlic, and 2 tablespoons of the sesame oil. Slide your hand between the chicken flesh and the skin on the breast and legs to separate the skin a little. Rub the oil mixture under the skin, spreading over the entire bird.

Mix the lemon juice and sherry. Pour over the exterior of the chicken skin. Sprinkle the bird with salt and pepper.

Roll the heads of garlic on the countertop to the separate the cloves slightly. Cut off the top of each bulb. Drizzle the remaining tablespoon of sesame oil over the garlic, dividing the oil between the 4 bulbs. Wrap the 4 bulbs together in foil.

Place the chicken in a shallow roasting pan and bake it and the garlic (place the foil package of garlic on the oven rack) for 1 hour or until the chicken juices come out clear when you pierce the side of the breast. Let the chicken sit for 15 minutes before slicing.

Serve the chicken sliced with 1 head of roasted garlic per person. Spread the garlic on bites of chicken as you eat.

Serves 4.

Sesame oil is an acquired taste—admittedly, many people never acquire it. The flavor of sesame oil can be somewhat overpowering; using it in place of olive oil presents a certain risk. Usually, recipes call for only $^1/_2$–1 teaspoon of sesame oil at a time. Often, it is combined with more acidic ingredients to balance its dark, nutty characteristics. That said, I still love to use more sesame oil in my cooking at times to achieve unusual flavors.

CHILI-CHOCOLATE CHICKEN SATAY WITH PEANUT-CUCUMBER RELISH

Satay:

- 1 tablespoon chili pepper sauce, such as Tabasco or Louisiana hot sauce
- 4 tablespoons cocoa powder
- 3/4 teaspoon cumin
- 1 clove garlic, crushed
- 1/4 teaspoon cinnamon
- 1/4 cup minced fresh cilantro leaves
- 2 tablespoons honey
- 1/4 cup dry sherry
- 1/2 teaspoon salt
- 1 pound boneless, skinless chicken breast, sliced into long 1-inch-wide strips

Relish:

- 1/4 cup chunky peanut butter
- 1 teaspoon sesame oil
- 1 teaspoon red chili sauce
- 1 tablespoon rice wine vinegar
- 1/2 cup peeled, seeded, diced cucumber
- 4 scallions, diced
- 1 clove garlic, crushed
- 1/4 cup minced fresh cilantro leaves
- 1/8 teaspoon cinnamon
- 1/2 teaspoon cumin

In a sealable container, combine all the satay ingredients except the chicken, stirring well. Drop the chicken strips into the marinade and stir so all the chicken is covered in sauce. Refrigerate for at least 2 hours and up to 24 hours.

Soak 20 wooden skewers in water for approximately 20 minutes.

Skewer each piece of chicken; the skewer should pass through the chicken strip 2 or 3 times. Grill over hot coals or under a broiler for about 4 minutes per side or until just done. Do not overcook or the chicken will be tough.

Combine all the ingredients for the peanut-cucumber relish, stirring well. Serve with the satay.

Serves 4.

This recipe is a version of a common Thai dish—Chicken Satay with Peanut Sauce. It's an example of how wild one can be in combining flavors of different cultures with delicious results. If anything, Rocky Mountain gourmet food means blending cultural and regional ingredients with no fear of the unknown. I've added some distinctly Rocky Mountain ingredients to give this particular blend even more pizazz.

ORANGE TEA DUCK

2 cups freshly brewed Black Pekoe tea
1 cup orange juice
$1/2$ teaspoon grated lemon zest
1 teaspoon grated fresh ginger root
1 clove garlic, crushed
3 tablespoons honey
$1/2$ teaspoon salt
1 tablespoon sesame oil
$1/4$ teaspoon cinnamon
$1/8$ teaspoon cayenne pepper
1 whole duck with the skin on, cleaned

Mix all the ingredients except the duck in a medium saucepan. Heat to boiling.

Place the duck in a shallow baking dish. Pour the tea mixture over the duck, turning the duck several times so all of it gets some marinade. Cover the dish with a lid or foil and refrigerate overnight (or up to 48 hours for a richer flavor), turning the duck several times in its marinade.

Preheat the oven to 375°.

Bake the duck in the sauce, covered, for 30 minutes, turning once. Remove the pan from the oven.

Increase the oven temperature to 425°. Place the duck on a rack over a baking sheet. Roast the duck for an additional 15 minutes, until it is crispy and browned.

Meanwhile, pour the sauce from the baking dish into a small saucepan and simmer over medium heat until it is reduced to $3/4$ cup.

Slice the duck and serve it with the sauce. Serves 2–4.

One of the tricks of preparing duck well is to leave it as rare as possible—don't let it dry out. Many chefs wrap duck in bacon while cooking it in order to keep the duck meat moist. My strategy is always to simply cook duck to rare. I don't have to worry about typical slaughterhouse bacteria; my duck meat often comes from family and friends who have recently butchered their game with deliberate care—another benefit of hunting, or of dining with those who do.

QUAIL WITH FENNEL AND TARRAGON CREAM

2 tablespoons olive oil

4 quail, domestic or wild, split and opened so they lie flat—or substitute 2 Cornish Game Hens

1 clove garlic, crushed

4 shallots, minced

1 cup chopped fresh fennel bulb

½ cup dry white wine

1 cup heavy cream

1 tablespoon fresh tarragon

½ teaspoon salt

⅛ teaspoon black pepper

Heat the oil in a large non-stick skillet over medium-high heat. Brown the quail until golden, about 3–5 minutes on each side. Remove the birds to a waiting platter.

Sauté the garlic, shallots, and fennel in the same pan for 8–10 minutes or until softened. Add the wine and cook for 3 minutes, until partially reduced. Add the cream, tarragon, salt, and black pepper and stir to combine. Simmer for 5 minutes.

Return the quail to the pan and simmer for 10 minutes, spooning the sauce over the birds. Serve over rice or couscous.

Serves 2.

I still dream about a dish similar to this one that I had at the Double Arrow Ranch in Seeley, Montana. The historic one-time dude ranch, now a cozy resort, serves excellent examples of Rocky Mountain gourmet food. Quail aren't found in the northern Rockies due to cold temperatures, so I was delighted to get a taste of this delicate fowl. It was paired with a buffalo tenderloin in wild mushroom port sauce; but the quail were treated with the gentle hand they require and were served in a basil cream sauce. My version of this delightful dish adds the licorice flavors of fennel and tarragon. Check the appendix (Resources for Special Rocky Mountain Ingredients) to assist you in your efforts to find farm-raised game birds like pheasant, quail, and duck.

BRAISED GROUSE MARSALA

4 tablespoons flour

¼ teaspoon salt

¼ teaspoon black pepper

2 grouse, cut into serving pieces—or substitue
Cornish Game Hens

6 tablespoons butter

4 tablespoons finely minced onion

1 cup sliced white or crimini mushrooms

½ teaspoon fresh rosemary, crumbled

1 teaspoon grated lemon zest

¾ cup marsala

1 cup chicken stock

Combine the flour, salt, and pepper in a small bowl. Dredge the pieces of grouse in this mixture.

Melt the butter in a large non-stick skillet over medium-high heat. Brown the grouse pieces on both sides, about 5 minutes per side. Remove the grouse to a platter and set aside.

Add the onion, mushrooms, rosemary, lemon zest, and 1 tablespoon of the dredging flour to the skillet and sauté for 8 minutes. Whisk in the marsala and broth and stir until smooth and thickened.

Return the grouse to the skillet and braise for 15 minutes. Season with salt and pepper to taste. Serve over pasta or rice.

Serves 2.

Suggested Menu:

- Dried Mushroom Caviar with sliced baguette (page 15)
- Zucchini Buttermilk Soup (page 37)
- Braised Grouse Marsala
- Petite Peas with Prosciutto and Garlic (page 60)
- Cheddar Biscuits with Thyme and Sage (page 161)
- Raspberry-Rhubarb Sorbet (page 127)

Low Fat

THREE PEPPER PENNE WITH CHICKEN

1 pound dry penne pasta, cooked and drained

2 teaspoons olive oil

½ cup diced onion

2 cloves garlic, crushed

1 pound boneless, skinless chicken breast, cut into bite-sized strips

1 red bell pepper, seeded and julienned

2 jalapeños, seeded and diced

¼ cup minced fresh basil leaves

½ teaspoon red pepper flakes

¼ cup white wine

1 15-ounce can Italian-style stewed tomatoes, diced, with the juice

salt and pepper to taste

freshly grated Parmesan cheese for garnish

Toss the cooked and drained pasta with 1 teaspoon of the olive oil, coating the pasta well.

Heat the second teaspoon of olive oil in a skillet over medium-high heat. Sauté the onion and garlic for 3 minutes, until the onion begins to soften. Add the chicken pieces to the pan and stir for about 5 minutes, slightly browning the chicken. Add the remaining ingredients and stir to combine. Continue cooking for about 10 minutes, until the sauce is bubbling.

Toss the sauce over the penne pasta and serve immediately, garnished with freshly grated Parmesan cheese.

Serves 4.

Packed with more vitamin C for their weight than any other fruit or vegetable—including oranges and lemons—peppers seem like nature's perfect health food. And you get to choose among hot, medium, and mild.

FISH AND SEAFOOD

Green Chili- and Corn-Stuffed Trout with Lime

Trout in Parchment with Lemon and Julienned Vegetables

Sea Bass in Cashew Crust with Gingered Apricot Sauce

Tri-color Seafood Lasagne

Corn-Husk-Wrapped Salmon with Chipotle Lime Butter

Sage- and Pine Nut-Crusted Trout with Rosehip Wine Cream

Oysters and Walnuts En Croute with Sherry Sauce

Pine-Planked Salmon with Thai Basil Oil

Citrus Chili Barbecued Northern Pike

Perch in Coconut Ginger Beer Batter

Pickled Shrimp and Fish in Lettuce Packages

Sturgeon in Creamy Ceasar Sauce

Low Fat

GREEN CHILI- AND CORN-STUFFED TROUT WITH LIME

Sauce:
1 clove garlic, crushed
1 cup white wine
juice of 1 fresh lime
2 teaspoons cornstarch
¼ teaspoon cumin
⅛ teaspoon cayenne pepper
salt and pepper to taste
1 tablespoon granulated sugar

Stuffing:
1 7-ounce can green chilies, diced

1 cup frozen sweet corn or fresh-cut corn from the cob
¼ cup minced fresh cilantro leaves
3 scallions, diced, including tops
½ teaspoon cumin
¼ teaspoon salt
¼ teaspoon pepper
¼ teaspoon oregano
¼ cup bread crumbs

Fish:
4 whole trout, about 10–12 inches long, cleaned and scaled
1 lime

Combine all the sauce ingredients in a small saucepan. Whisk over medium heat until smooth and thickened, about 5–8 minutes. Keep warm on low for later use.

Preheat the oven to 375°.

Combine the stuffing ingredients in a mixing bowl and stir well. Divide the stuffing between the 4 fish, pressing it firmly into the fish cavities until it forms a smooth mound on the outside. Wrap the fish individually in foil or place them on a baking sheet and cover with foil. Bake for 20 minutes. Uncover the fish, squeeze lime juice over them, and bake for an additional 8 minutes to brown.

Spoon the sauce onto 4 dinner plates and lay a stuffed fish in the middle of each.

Serves 4.

From the Saddle Ridge Clubhouse Restaurant in Beaver Creek, Colorado, to the River Grille in Jackson, Wyoming, to Bucks T-4 near Big Sky Resort, Montana, the number of menus that feature trout is growing. While you'll often see wild trout listed on Rocky Mountain restaurant menus, "wild" does not mean the trout were caught in a raging river nearby. True wild game cannot be prepared for sale, so the trout served in restaurants are farm raised.

Low
Fat

TROUT IN PARCHMENT WITH LEMON AND JULIENNED VEGETABLES

¼ cup julienned carrot

¼ cup julienned celery

¼ cup julienned zucchini

¼ cup julienned red bell pepper

¼ cup julienned red onion

1 clove garlic, crushed

1 teaspoon thyme

½ teaspoon marjoram

2 tablespoons minced fresh dill

4 whole trout, about 6–8 inches long, cleaned and scaled with the heads and tails removed

4 sheets of parchment paper cut into large heart shapes big enough to enclose the fish

4 tablespoons dry sherry

salt and pepper to taste

1 fresh lemon, sliced in thin rounds

Preheat the oven to 435°.

Combine the vegetables, garlic, and herbs in a mixing bowl.

Lay each fish on one side of a heart-shaped parchment. Stuff the vegetable mixture into the fish cavities, dividing it evenly among the 4 fish. Sprinkle 1 tablespoon of sherry over each vegetable stuffing mound; salt and pepper stuffing to taste. Press down on the fish to re-flatten them. Lay lemon slices across the exterior skin of each fish. Fold the parchments in half over the fish, crimping the edges to competely enclose the fish.

Place the 4 wrapped fish on a baking sheet. Bake for 20–25 minutes, depending on the thickness of the fish.

Arrange the fish on dinner plates. Slit the paper open down the center just as the fish are served.

You can stuff and wrap the fish up to 12 hours ahead of time; refrigerate them until you are ready to bake. Add an additional 8 minutes to the baking time if the fish are chilled.

Serves 4.

In addition to the inherent simplicity of baking a fish whole (i.e., in its skin with no fillet knife performance required), here are several other reasons to cook trout this way: The flavor is exquisite, since cooking a trout whole prevents the fish from drying out. Fewer juices leak out during the cooking process, because the oil in the skin makes the fish self-basting and seals the whole works perfectly. And a whole trout presented on the table brings back pleasant memories of a day on the river.

SEA BASS IN CASHEW CRUST WITH GINGERED APRICOT SAUCE

Crust:
- ½ cup unsalted, roasted cashew nuts
- 3 tablespoons all-purpose flour
- 1 teaspoon paprika
- salt and pepper to taste

Fish:
- 2 sea bass fillets, 8–10 ounces each
- 1 egg, slightly beaten
- non-stick cooking spray

Sauce:
- ½ cup unsweetened all-fruit apricot jam
- ½ cup rice wine or white wine
- 2 tablespoons grated fresh ginger
- 1 tablespoon teriyaki sauce
- 1 tablespoon Dijon mustard

Combine the crust ingredients in a blender or food processor. Chop in pulses until the cashews are coarsely ground. Pour the mixture onto a plate.

Lay the bass fillets in the beaten egg, coating both sides. Dredge the egg-dipped fish in the crust mixture, pressing the breading into the flesh of the fish.

Coat a non-stick skillet with cooking spray and heat to medium-high on the stovetop. Lay the fillets in the pan. Spray the tops of the fillets with cooking spray, too. Brown the fillets for 7 minutes on one side. Turn them over and cover the skillet. Brown for another 7–10 minutes, depending on the thickness of the fish. Pull the center of the fish flesh apart to ensure that the fillet is opaque all the way through.

While the fillets are browning, combine all the sauce ingredients in a small saucepan over medium heat, stirring until blended and hot.

Serve the sauce over the fillets.

Serves 2.

I was introduced to nut-encrusted fish at the **Fly Fisher's Inn** near the Dearborn River Valley in Montana, where this preparation is a regular menu item. Crusting a fish may sound like a bit of trouble, but for a special meal it's worth the effort. There's not a nut that can't be used as a delicious crust for fish, chicken, or even beef. The oil in the nuts makes them brown well against the surface of the flesh, helping to seal in the juices. A blender—or better yet, a food processor—makes crust preparation a breeze, but a sharp knife and some elbow grease also work just fine. Add a lighter, binding ingredient like bread crumbs, bran, or flour to help the ground nuts stick, and some herbs and spices to complement the sweet flavors of the nuts and meat. See page 111 for ingredient suggestions.

TRI-COLOR SEAFOOD LASAGNE

4 tablespoons butter

¼ cup finely diced onion

2 cloves garlic, crushed

4 tablespoons flour

1 cup white wine

3 cups half-and-half

1 teaspoon salt

¼ teaspoon black pepper

¼ cup chopped fresh basil leaves

1 10-ounce package frozen chopped spinach, thawed and drained

4 sheets each of red pepper, spinach, and plain lasagne noodles, cooked and drained

½ pound crab flakes

1 pound ricotta cheese

3 cups grated mozzarella cheese

1½ cups freshly grated Parmesan cheese

1 pound red snapper fillets, cubed

2 cups prepared tomato marinara sauce

¾ pound small- to medium-sized raw shrimp, peeled

non-stick cooking spray

Preheat the oven to 375°.

Melt the butter in a medium-sized saucepan over medium heat. Sauté the onion and garlic for 5 minutes. Stir in the flour and cook for 2 minutes. Whisk in the white wine. As the mixture begins to thicken, whisk in the half-and-half. Stir constantly until the sauce is smooth and thickened, about 3–5 minutes. Stir in the salt and pepper and remove from the heat.

Pour half the sauce into a medium-sized bowl. Add the fresh basil and spinach to make a green sauce. Stir well to combine.

Coat the bottom of a deep lasagne pan with cooking spray. Spread a spoonful of the white sauce over the bottom of the pan. Lay the 4 spinach lasagne noodles lengthwise across the pan, overlapping the edges if necessary. Arrange the crab flakes to cover the noodles. Spread all of the green sauce on top.

Combine the ricotta, mozzarella, and Parmesan cheeses in a bowl, mixing well.

Spread a third of the cheese mixture over the green sauce in the pan. Add a layer of plain white lasagne noodles. Arrange the raw red snapper over the white noodles. Spread the the rest of the plain cream sauce over the fish and top with another third of the cheese. Cover the cheese layer with the 4 red pepper noodles. Arrange the shrimp over the pasta and spread the marinara sauce over the shrimp. Cover with the last third of the cheese.

Bake for 45 minutes or until browned and bubbly.

Serves 8.

When I was teaching a lowfat gourmet class one winter in Great Falls, Montana, I came up with a lighter version of this recipe that used nonfat cheese products. It was delicious, as nonfat cheese dishes go, and I decided the idea was good, but not always called for. So, this recipe can be prepared two ways, rich or light, with the choice of whole milk or skim milk products, depending on your company and your taste.

CORN-HUSK-WRAPPED SALMON WITH CHIPOTLE-LIME BUTTER

7–13 pieces of dried corn husk, soaked in hot water for 20 minutes, or fresh whole husks with the silk removed

6 6–8-ounce salmon fillets, each cut lengthwise down the center and the 2 halves stacked on top of each other

6 tablespoons melted butter

1 teaspoon grated lime peel

1 tablespoon lime juice

1–2 tablespoons puréed canned chipotle chilies in adobo sauce

1 clove garlic, crushed

¼ cup minced cilantro leaves

salt and pepper to taste

Lay the moist corn husks on a flat surface (reserving 1 for later use) and arrange 2 strips of salmon filet (1 on top of the other) down the center of each. Use the 6 largest corn husks you can find—those that will completely enclose the fish—or use 12 smaller ones, placing 2 husks side-by-side and overlapping the edges.

Stir the butter, lime rind, lime juice, chilies, garlic, cilantro, salt, and pepper together in a small mixing bowl. Spoon this mixture over the top fillets, spreading the seasoning around. Fold the sides of the husks completely over the salmon and use ½-inch-wide strips cut from the extra husk to tie off both ends of each husk, so they look like firecrackers.

Cook the husks for about 15 minutes, either in a steamer, in a 375° oven, or over coals. Serve on individual plates, allowing the guests to unwrap their own salmon.

Serves 6.

The traditional packaging for the Mexican tamales I adore, corn husks work like parchment paper to hold the flavor of the enclosed ingredients in close to the food. The earthy presentation of the corn husk and the flavor it infuses into the salmon make this my favorite wrapping for fish and poultry.

The most flavorful way to cook the husks is on the barbecue grill. If the husks are charring too quickly, just brush some lime water over the surfaces of the husks three or four times during grilling. It's best to use fresh husks, straight out of your garden, with an ear of corn served beside each husk-wrapped salmon fillet. The dried husks you can find in the Mexican section of most grocery stores work fine, too. Dried husks must be soaked before using. Try some corn-husk-wrapped packages of vegetables (zucchini, carrot sticks, bell peppers in a variety of colors) on the grill with the salmon for a fun meal.

SAGE- AND PINE NUT–CRUSTED TROUT WITH ROSEHIP WINE CREAM

Crust:

- ³⁄₄ cup fine dry bread crumbs
- ¹⁄₄ cup cornmeal
- ¹⁄₂ cup pine nuts
- ¹⁄₂ teaspoon sage
- ¹⁄₄ teaspoon black pepper
- ¹⁄₂ teaspoon salt

Fish:

- 3 tablespoons vegetable oil
- 6 trout fillets, about 8–10 ounces each
- 2 eggs, lightly beaten

Cream Sauce:

- 2 tablespoons butter
- 2 teaspoons flour
- 4 tablespoons rosehip powder (see page 50 for preparation directions)
- 1 cup white wine
- 2 tablespoons orange juice concentrate
- 1 cup half-and-half
- ¹⁄₄ cup rosehip pieces, seedless
- ¹⁄₄ teaspoon salt
- ¹⁄₈ teaspoon cayenne pepper

  cucumber peelings, stripped off with vegetable peeler and soaked in ice water until they curl

Combine the crust ingredients in a food processor or blender. Process in pulses until the pine nuts are coarsely chopped.

Heat 1 tablespoon of the oil over medium-high heat in a large non-stick skillet. Dip the trout fillets in the beaten egg then dredge them in the crust mixture. Lay 2 at a time in the skillet. Brown for 5 minutes on 1 side. Turn and brown on the other side for 3–5 minutes. Place the browned fillets in an ovenproof pan. Brown the other 2 batches of fillets, using 1 tablespoon of oil for each batch. Keep them warm in a 200° oven while preparing the sauce.

To prepare the sauce, melt the butter in a small saucepan over medium heat. Add the flour and rosehip powder and stir constantly for 2 minutes. Whisk the wine and orange juice into this mixture until it is smooth and beginning to thicken. Then whisk the half-and-half into the pan, stirring until

smooth. Add the rosehip pieces to the sauce and simmer for 10–15 minutes, until the rosehip pieces soften.

Spoon the sauce onto 6 dinner plates and lay a trout fillet on top of the sauce on each plate. Garnish with cucumber curls.

Serves 6.

Try some of these other nut crusts for variety with your fish: peanuts with cornmeal and thyme; pecans with whole wheat flour, cinnamon, and cayenne; and macadamia nuts with dried papaya and ginger. Try to keep your fillet-flipping to a minimum, giving the nuts less chance to fall off.

OYSTERS AND WALNUTS EN CROUTE WITH SHERRY SAUCE

4 tablespoons butter
1 cup sliced crimini or white mushrooms
$1/4$ cup finely diced onion
$1/4$ cup finely diced celery
$1/4$ cup finely diced carrot
1 clove garlic, crushed
3 tablespoons flour
1 cup vegetable or fish stock
4 tablespoons dry sherry
1 cup half-and-half
$1/4$ teaspoon marjoram
$1/8$ teaspoon sage

$1/2$ teaspoon thyme
$1/2$ teaspoon salt
$1/4$ teaspoon black pepper
2 tablespoons butter, melted
8 sheets phyllo dough
4 cups oysters in their liquid
$1/2$ cup walnut pieces
1 cup freshly grated Parmesan cheese

diced ripe tomatoes for garnish

Melt the butter in a non-stick skillet over medium heat. Sauté the mushrooms, vegetables, and garlic in the butter until they are soft, about 10 minutes. If they begin to brown, turn the heat down. Stir in the flour and cook for 2 minutes to dissolve well. Whisk in the stock and sherry and simmer until the sauce is smooth and thickened. Whisk in the half-and-half, herbs, salt, and pepper and continue to simmer until smooth and bubbly. Remove from heat and set aside.

Preheat the oven to 400°.

Brush 4 ovenproof individual serving dishes or casseroles (2-cup capacity) with butter. Lay $1/2$ sheet of phyllo in each. Brush with butter and cover with another $1/2$ sheet. Repeat 2 more times until you have 4 half sheets in each serving dish. Press the phyllo into the dishes and trim the edges to within $1/2$ inch of the edge of each dish.

Add the oysters and their liquid to the sauce and stir for 1 minute. Then ladle oyster sauce onto the phyllo dough in each of the serving dishes,

dividing it among the 4 dishes. Top with the walnut pieces. Sprinkle $1/4$ cup of Parmesan over each bowl or casserole.

Bake until bubbly and browning on top, about 12–15 minutes. Serve immediately, garnished with diced tomatoes.

Serves 4.

Suggested Menu:

- Huckleberry Brie En Croute (page 16)
- Feta- and Lemon-Crumb Stuffed Artichokes (page 61)
- Oysters and Walnuts En Croute with Sherry Sauce
- Walnut, Garlic, and Sun-dried Tomato Foccacia (page 159)
- Taos Cinnamon-Chocolate Torte (page 121)

PINE-PLANKED SALMON
WITH THAI BASIL OIL

Thai Basil Oil:

4 tablespoons vegetable oil

1 tablespoon hot chili-sesame oil

¼ cup minced basil leaves

juice of ½ fresh lime

1 clove garlic, crushed

Fish:

2-inch-thick x 6-inch-wide plank
    of untreated pine wood,
    about 1½ feet long

olive oil for brushing the wood

½ lime

salt and pepper to taste

4 8-ounce salmon fillets

Combine the ingredients for the basil oil in a food processor or blender and process until puréed. Set aside.

Lay the plank of wood in a plugged sink and pour boiling water over it, turning to soak both sides. Let it soak in the hot water for about 20 minutes, turning a couple of times. Drain the water and place the plank over a baking sheet in the oven. Set the oven on 400° and heat the wet pine plank for 20 minutes or until you begin to smell the pine sap rising. Remove the plank and brush it with olive oil on one side. Return it to the oven for 5 minutes.

Sprinkle lime juice, salt, and black pepper over both sides of the salmon fillets. Lay the fillets on the oiled side of the plank. Return to the 400° oven and bake for 10–15 minutes, depending on the thickness of the fillets.

Remove the whole plank from the oven. Immediately brush the fillets with Thai Basil Oil. Lay the plank with the fish on it right in the center of the serving table, balancing it on a trivet or 2 flat rocks.

Serves 4.

I once saw a vintage menu from the historic Montana Hotel, built in Anaconda by copper king Marcus Daly in 1888. The hotel's 1899 New Year's Eve dinner menu featured a planked whitefish entree. I was surprised to see this dish alongside very traditional fare like Prime Rib Au Jus and Capon in Oyster Sauce—I thought planked fish was a contemporary preparation.

Another time, I met a woman in a cooking store (she seemed as enthralled with the different devices for shucking corn as I was that day) and we somehow ended up discussing planked fish. She encouraged me to work on creating a well-seasoned fish plank, in much the same way one might season a pot with continuous cooking over time. She suggested I find out which wood I liked best, then use the same plank over and over until the wood developed gourmet status as a fish-cooking treasure. She claimed that flavors develop in a piece of wood over time; that the longer the same plank is used, the better the fish cooked on it would be. But, after much experimentation, I have found that the piney pitch or cedar flavors are strongest in the wood the first time I cook on it.

Low Fat

CITRUS CHILI BARBECUED NORTHERN PIKE

1 teaspoon vegetable oil

1/2 cup diced red onion

2 cloves garlic, crushed

2 tablespoons orange juice concentrate

3 tablespoons lime juice

3/4 cup ketchup

1/4–1/2 teaspoon cayenne pepper

2 tablespoons soy sauce

1/4 cup red wine

2–4 drops smoked seasoning liquid

4–6 pike fillets

Heat the oil in a small saucepan over medium heat. Sauté the onion and garlic for 5 minutes. Add the remaining ingredients to the pan, except the fish. Simmer on low heat for 15–20 minutes, until the sauce is smooth and thickened.

Preheat the oven to 425°.

Dip the fish fillets in the sauce and place them on a rack over a baking sheet. Bake for about 15–20 minutes. Or, grill the fish on an outdoor grill for 12–15 minutes, turning halfway through cooking. Test the center of one fillet for doneness: pull the flesh apart with a knife and make sure center is opaque. Serve over rice with additional sauce on the side for dipping.

Serves 4–6.

When my dad brought me some luscious, firm, mild northern pike from his fishing trip to Canada's Northern Rockies, I created this sauce. I especially enjoy grilling freshwater pike this way and serving it on a bed of fresh spinach leaves, topped with the Jicama Citrus Salad with Red Peppers (page 41). Double or quadruple the sauce recipe and keep it in the refrigerator for up to 12 days to baste a variety of fish, poultry, and other meats, or freeze it for quick reheating.

PERCH IN COCONUT-GINGER BEER BATTER

Fish:

10 tablespoons all-purpose flour

4 tablespoons cornmeal

1 teaspoon ground ginger

¼ teaspoon cayenne pepper

½ teaspoon salt

½ teaspoon baking powder

¼ cup flaked coconut

¾ cup beer

½ cup vegetable oil

4 perch fillets

Ginger Mayonnaise Sauce:

1 cup mayonnaise

2 tablespoons lemon juice

½ teaspoon ground ginger

⅛ teaspoon cayenne pepper

Combine the flour, cornmeal, ginger, cayenne, salt, baking powder, and coconut in a small mixing bowl. Pour the beer into the dry ingredients and mix until smooth.

Heat the oil in a skillet over medium-high heat.

Dip both sides of the perch fillets in the batter and slide into the oil. Fry the fish for about 5 minutes or until golden on one side. Turn them over and fry the other side until golden.

Whisk all the sauce ingredients together and serve as a dip with the perch.

Serves 4.

Since it opened in 1901, Boise's elegant Idanha Hotel has served its garden city a carefully planned regional menu. At its restaurant, Peter Schotts's new American cuisine provides locals and visitors to this lively city an adventure in dining. The menu does a delicious job with the Rocky Mountain gourmet theme. Schotts includes the flavors that predominate in his community and highlights the catch of the day with exciting flavors like the ones in this recipe.

PICKLED SHRIMP AND FISH
IN LETTUCE PACKAGES

Pickled Shrimp and Fish:

$1/3$	cup rice wine vinegar
$1/4$	cup lemon juice
$1/8$	cup soy sauce
3	tablespoons hot pepper sesame oil
1	clove garlic, crushed
1	tablespoon grated fresh ginger
1	tablespoon brown sugar
1	pound peeled small to medium-sized raw shrimp
$3/4$	pound firm white fish fillets, sliced into 1-inch chunks

Lettuce Packages:

16–20	whole butter lettuce leaves or red leaf lettuce leaves, separated from the head
3	cups sticky Asian-style rice, cooked and cooled
5	scallions, diced
4	tablespoons toasted sesame seeds
	toothpicks

Combine all the ingredients for the pickled shrimp and fish in a sealable container. Shake well to blend the flavors and refrigerate overnight.

Pour the entire contents of the refrigerated container into a wok or skillet. Sauté on medium-high heat for 3–5 minutes or until the shrimp turn pink. With a slotted spoon, remove the fish and shrimp to a separate bowl.

Continue to simmer the marinade for another 5 minutes. Pour this liquid back over the shrimp and fish and refrigerate for 2–6 more hours.

To assemble the lettuce packages, lay several lettuce leaves on a flat surface. Heap 4 spoonfuls of rice into the center of each leaf. Flatten the rice with the back of a spoon. Sprinkle chopped scallion and sesame seeds over the rice and top with several pieces of fish and shrimp. When you are dividing the ingredients among the lettuce leaves, keep in mind that you will be making 16–20 packages.

Fold the sides of each lettuce leaf over the filling, as if you were wrapping a package. Secure each package with a toothpick through the center.

Repeat with another batch of leaves, until you've used up all the filling ingredients.

Lay the lettuce packages in a shallow pan. Use a small spoon to drizzle the remaining sauce over the packages. Refrigerate until ready to serve. Serve 3 or 4 lettuce packages to each person.

Serves 4–6, depending on the number of packages you made.

Suggested Menu:

- **Trout Cakes with Rosehip Citrus Mayonnaise (page 8)**
- **Pickled Shrimp and Fish in Lettuce Packages**
- **Steamed Carrots and Zucchini with Chipotle Chili Butter (page 63)**
- **Tassajara Bread (page 146)**
- **Dried Apple–Whole Wheat Charlotte (page 125)**

STURGEON IN CREAMY CAESAR SAUCE

Fish:
- 1 cup white wine
- 2 tablespoons lemon juice
- 1 clove garlic, crushed
- 1/4 teaspoon thyme
- 4 1 1/4–1 1/2-inch-thick sturgeon steaks, skinned

Sauce:
- 1 tablespoon extra virgin olive oil
- 1 tablespoon anchovy paste
- 2 cloves garlic, crushed
- 3 tablespoons lemon juice
- 1 cup white wine

- 2 egg yolks at room temperature, slightly beaten in a small bowl
- 1/2 cup grated fresh Parmesan cheese
- 1/4 teaspoon black pepper
- 1/2 teaspoon salt
- 2 scallions, finely diced
- 1/2 cup heavy cream

chopped parsley and grated Parmesan for garnish

Measure the wine and lemon juice into a large skillet over medium heat. Add the garlic and thyme and bring to a slow boil.

Lay the sturgeon steaks in the liquid in the skillet and cook them for 10 minutes. Turn the steaks over and braise for another 10 minutes. Cover the skillet and remove from the heat while preparing the Caesar sauce.

Heat the olive oil in a small saucepan over medium heat. Stir in the anchovy paste and the garlic and cook for 1–2 minutes to combine the flavors. Whisk in the lemon juice and white wine and simmer for about 3 minutes.

Whisk 1/4 cup of the anchovy-wine mixture into the egg yolks, beating until they turn lemon colored and the mixture is smooth. Slowly pour the egg yolk mixture into the saucepan, whisking constantly. Continue whisking until the sauce is thickened and smooth. Stir in the Parmesan cheese, black pepper, salt, scallions, and cream. Simmer for another 3–5 minutes and remove from the heat.

Using a slotted spatula, lift the steaks from the braising liquid to the dinner plates. Spoon the Creamy Caesar Sauce on top and garnish with additional grated Parmesan and parsley.

Serves 4.

Very firm and less flaky in texture than many fish, sturgeon is especially easy to cook with. Sturgeon fillets are wonderful grilled on a barbecue with garlic, peppers, and ginger. You can use more vibrantly flavored sauces with sturgeon, since the flavor of the fish is not easily masked.

DESSERTS

Brandied Rhubarb Custard Cobbler

Taos Cinnamon–Chocolate Torte

Spiced Banana Egg Rolls with Frozen Yogurt

Cowboy Coffee Sauce

Ginger Oatmeal Cake

Dried Apple–Whole Wheat Charlotte

Chocolate Mocha Biscotti

Raspberry–Rhubarb Sorbet

Pecan Bizcochitos

Huckleberry Bread Pudding

Flathead Cherry Fudge Torte

Spiced Native American Blue Corn Pudding

Apple Tart Tatin

Finnish Golden Raisin–Almond Cake

Dried Cherry– and Chocolate–Studded Gingerbread Cake

German Sour Cream Pastry Twists

Musher's Cream Cheese Shortbread Cookies

Cardamom–Port Flan

Pine Nut Brittle

Apple Dumplings Stuffed with Cranberries and Walnuts in Whiskey Syrup

Rocky Triple Nut Cheesecake

Merlot– and Honey–Poached Pears with Cinnamon Ricotta

Huckleberry Bittersweet Chocolate Truffles

Mexican Chocolate Mocha Fondue

BRANDIED RHUBARB CUSTARD COBBLER

Cobbler:
- 1 cup sugar
- 1/8 cup flour
- 5 cups sliced rhubarb
- 1/4 cup apricot brandy
- 2 1/2 cups half-and-half or whole milk
- 1/2 teaspoon cinnamon
- 1/8 teaspoon cloves
- 1/8 teaspoon nutmeg
- 1 teaspoon vanilla extract
- 3 eggs plus 2 egg yolks

Topping:
- 1 cup old-fashioned rolled oats
- 1 cup flour
- 1/2 teaspoon cinnamon
- 1 cup brown sugar
- 1/2 cup butter, melted

Preheat the oven to 350°. Grease a 6-cup glass baking dish or 6 individual custard cups.

In a medium-sized saucepan, pour the sugar and flour over the rhubarb and mix. Add the brandy and 1 1/2 cups of the half-and-half or milk. Put the mixture over medium heat and bring to a slow boil, stirring well. Cook for 2–3 minutes, until the mixture is smooth and begins to thicken. Remove from the heat and set aside.

Whisk the last cup of half-and-half or milk, the spices, vanilla, eggs, and egg yolks together in a medium-sized mixing bowl.

Stir 1/2 cup of the hot rhubarb into the egg mixture to temper it, then add the remaining rhubarb to the egg mixture, mixing to combine. Pour into the greased baking dish or custard cups.

Combine the topping ingredients in a bowl until moist and crumbly. Sprinkle the topping evenly over the custard. Place the baking dish in a larger pan and fill the pan with hot water halfway up the outside of the baking dish. If you are using individual custard cups, place them in an oblong cake pan and fill pan with hot water halfway up the outside of the custard cups.

Bake for 40–50 minutes or until the custard is set and not runny in the middle when tested with a knife.

Serves 6.

It only makes sense to call rhubarb—with its tall, celery-like stalks and leaves the size of your face or larger—a vegetable. But somewhere along the line, it got nudged into the fruit category. It is now typically found in fruit-centered recipes. You need about twice as much sugar as rhubarb to make the plant edible. My Grandma Mares could bake a mean rhubarb-custard pie, and her pie inspired this cobbler.

TAOS CINNAMON-CHOCOLATE TORTE

Torte:

- 1/2 cup ground almonds
- 1/4 cup flour
- 1/2 cup firmly packed dark brown sugar
- 2 teaspoons cinnamon
- 3 tablespoons instant coffee granules
- 1/2 teaspoon salt, plus an extra pinch
- 6 ounces bittersweet chocolate, broken into small pieces
- 2 tablespoons Kahlua
- 2 teaspoons Mexican vanilla extract
- 5 large eggs, separated
- 1/4 cup granulated sugar

Glaze:

- 3 ounces bittersweet chocolate, chopped
- 2 tablespoons butter
- 2 teaspoons light corn syrup
- 2 tablespoons whipping cream

Preheat the oven to 350°. Grease an 8 1/2-inch springform pan and line the bottom with a circle of wax paper. Grease the paper and dust it with flour.

Combine the almonds, flour, brown sugar, cinnamon, instant coffee, 1/2 teaspoon salt, and chocolate in a food processor or blender. Process until the chocolate is finely ground.

Add the Kahlua, vanilla, and egg yolks to the chocolate mixture. Process until well combined and very thick. Scoop the mixture into a separate mixing bowl.

With an electric mixer, beat the egg whites with the pinch of salt until the mixture holds peaks. Add the granulated sugar and beat until stiff.

Whisk a third of the egg whites into the chocolate mixture, then gently fold in the remaining egg whites.

Pour the batter into the prepared pan. Bake for about 50 minutes or until a cake tester or toothpick inserted in the center comes out clean. Cool the torte on a rack for 10 minutes then remove the sides of the springform pan. Invert the torte onto the cooking rack, peel off the wax paper, and let the torte cool.

Combine all the glaze ingredients in a double boiler over low heat. Stir until melted and smooth. Cool to lukewarm and pour over the torte on the rack. (Place waxed paper underneath to catch the drippings.) Smooth the top with a spatula. Let the excess glaze drip down the sides.

Serves 8.

This recipe was inspired by a trip to the Taos Pueblo, New Mexico. My trips throughout the Rockies, along with taste-linked images of meals shared in the homes of family and friends, create the flavors, the combinations of textures and colors, and the cultural themes in my cooking. Sometimes I set out to mirror a taste I loved, but often my recipes are loosely inspired by the mood of a particular day.

Low Fat

SPICED BANANA EGG ROLLS WITH FROZEN YOGURT

¼ cup egg substitute or fat-free egg product

½ teaspoon vanilla

6 store-bought egg roll wrappers

1 cup lightly crushed bran flake cereal

½ teaspoon ground cinnamon

½ teaspoon ground ginger

6 whole bananas, peeled

nonfat frozen yogurt in vanilla, fruit, or coffee flavor

fresh raspberries and chocolate syrup or Cowboy Coffee Sauce for garnish

non-stick cooking spray

Preheat the oven to 400°. Coat a baking sheet with non-stick spray.

Mix the egg substitute and vanilla together in a small, shallow bowl.

In another shallow bowl, combine the bran flakes, cinnamon, and ginger.

Take the bananas through this process, one at a time: Roll in the egg mixture; wrap in an uncooked egg roll wrapper; roll in the egg mixture again; roll in the cereal mixture; place on the baking sheet.

Lightly spray the tops and sides of the bananas with the cooking spray. Place the baking sheet in oven and bake for about 8–12 minutes, until the bananas are browned and crisp.

Slice each banana in half with a slightly diagonal cut. Scoop yogurt into the center of each dessert plate and surround with three banana slices. Garnish with raspberries and drizzle with chocolate syrup or Cowboy Coffee Sauce (page 123).

Serves 4.

Sometimes a dessert is so unique or special that it should be given the place of honor in a meal. This dessert, high in flavor but low in fat, deserves that kind of glory. And, even though there are several steps to the recipe, it really is an easy one, especially since you forgo the deep-frying that traditional egg rolls require.

I like to prepare the simple but rich **Cowboy Coffee Sauce** on the next page to serve with ice cream, but it also looks and tastes wonderful drizzled over the yogurt and banana egg rolls in this dessert. You can also slice strips of mango or papaya and use them in place of the bananas, or in addition to the bananas. For a surprise in every egg roll, use all three fruits individually and put one of each on every plate.

Low
Fat

COWBOY COFFEE SAUCE

³/₄ cup leftover strong coffee
³/₄ cup brown sugar
 1 tablespoon brandy
¹/₂ teaspoon vanilla

In a medium-sized saucepan over medium-high heat, bring all the ingredients to a boil. Reduce the heat to prevent the syrup from boiling over, but continue to simmer for 10 minutes or until the mixture begins to thicken. Remove the syrup from the heat and let cool. Serve warm or refrigerate for up to 2 weeks.

Makes 1¹/₂ cups.

Cowhands of the West have always been known for their stout coffee, the kind with the grounds boiled in water for much longer than most of us would consider safe. And they rarely wasted a drop of this precious commodity. Leftover coffee was frequently used in gravy, poured over wild game or beef roast (as in the recipe for Coffee-Sage Roasted Elk on page 84), or used as a baking ingredient to add robust flavor to pound cakes. I always crave this coffee sauce on a frigid winter day—over ice cream, on pound cake, or even poured over flapjacks. It's simple to prepare and not a bad idea for a camping trip, if you don't want the weight of a bottle of pancake syrup in your pack. Just tuck some brown sugar in your backpack along with your coffee and your bottle (or tablespoon) of brandy.

GINGER OATMEAL CAKE

Cake:

1⅓ cups very hot water

1¼ cups old-fashioned rolled oats

1 tablespoon ground ginger

1 cup all-purpose unbleached white flour

⅓ cup whole wheat flour

1 teaspoon baking soda

1 teaspoon cinnamon

¼ teaspoon ground nutmeg

¾ teaspoon salt

1 cup firmly packed brown sugar

1 cup white sugar

⅓ cup margarine

2 large eggs

1 teaspoon vanilla

Icing:

¾ cup firmly packed brown sugar

4 tablespoons butter

¼ cup half-and-half

1 teaspoon vanilla

2 tablespoons whiskey, if desired

Preheat the oven to 350°. Grease a 9 x 13-inch baking pan.

Combine the hot water, oats, and ginger in a small bowl and let sit for 5 minutes. In another bowl, combine the flours, baking soda, cinnamon, nutmeg, and salt. Set aside.

In a large mixing bowl, beat the sugars and margarine together until fluffy. Add the eggs, one at a time, and the vanilla. Mix until everything is well incorporated.

Add the oat mixture to the egg mixture, stirring until smooth. Add the flour mixture, a third at a time, mixing until well combined.

Pour the batter into a greased cake pan and bake for 45 minutes or until a cake tester or toothpick inserted in center comes out clean.

While the cake cools, combine the icing ingredients in a medium-sized saucepan over medium-high heat. Bring to a boil and stir until the icing begins to thicken. While the icing is still warm, spread it over the cake in the pan.

Serves 8–12.

This old-fashioned oatmeal cake reminds me of how ingenious Rocky Mountain settlers were. They used whatever staples they had to make appealing meals that comforted them and filled their bellies after hard days of mining, logging, farming, ranching, hunting, or fishing. The physical isolation in which many early settlers lived meant they had to get by with rare trips to town for supplies. To survive, they made standard lists of staples not to be forgotten on these shopping trips. These lists show up in historic diaries, ledgers, and menus. They almost always include flour, oatmeal, lard, salt pork, dried apples, coffee beans, baking powder, salt, dry beans, sugar, and whiskey. People counted on the land to provide the rest of what they needed.

DRIED APPLE–WHOLE WHEAT CHARLOTTE

3 cups dried apple slices
6 tablespoons butter
1/4 cup sugar
1/2 cup apple juice
1 teaspoon cornstarch
1 tablespoon lemon juice
1 teaspoon finely grated lemon zest
1/2 teaspoon ground cinnamon

10 large slices of firm whole wheat bread
1/4 cup finely sliced almonds

In a saucepan over medium-high heat, combine the apples, 1 tablespoon of the butter, the sugar, apple juice, cornstarch, lemon juice, lemon zest, and cinnamon. Heat the mixture to boiling, stirring frequently. Reduce the heat to low, cover the pan, and continue to simmer for 35–45 minutes, stirring occasionally. You may need to add up to 1/2 cup of water if the mixture dries up. Remove the mixture from the heat and cool, or refrigerate overnight.

Preheat the oven to 375° to melt the remaining butter. Brush a 1-quart baking dish or a stainless steel or Pyrex bowl with a thin coat of butter.

Trim the crusts from the bread slices. Brush both sides of each slice with butter. Cut a large circle from the center of one slice and put it in the bottom of the baking bowl. Cut six of the bread slices in half lengthwise, making 12 rectangles. Arrange the halves like a pinwheel around the circle in the center of the bowl. Bend them up the sides of the bowl and overlap their edges. Slice another piece of bread into thirds to fit into the spaces between the bottom round and side pieces, to seal the bottom. Brush this bread lining with butter.

Stir the sliced almonds into the apple mixture.

Pour the filling into the bread-lined baking dish. Slice the remaining 2 pieces of bread and use them to cover the top of the apple charlotte, enclosing it completely. Brush with melted butter.

Bake for 30–40 minutes, until the top is well browned. Cool for 15 minutes, then unmold the charlotte by inverting it onto a plate. Serve with whipped cream or ice cream.

Serves 6–8.

Apple orchards are pretty common up and down the Rockies, from New Mexico to Idaho to Montana's Bitterroot Valley. Apples are easy to dry—you don't even need a food dehydrator. Peel the apples and dip 1/4-inch slices into a dish of water laced with lemon juice. Arrange the slices in single layers on kitchen-towel-covered cookie sheets. Put the pans in a 200° oven with the door cracked open. Let the apples dry for about 5 hours, until all the moisture is gone. You may need to turn them over once during the drying process. Let the apples dry out completely before storing them in airtight jars or plastic bags. If they are still moist after 5 hours, you can leave them in the cool oven overnight or cook them longer.

CHOCOLATE MOCHA BISCOTTI

3¼ cups all-purpose flour
2 cups sugar
1 teaspoon baking powder
½ teaspoon salt
5 large eggs
2 teaspoons vanilla
1 tablespoon water
½ cup cocoa powder
3 tablespoons instant coffee
½ cup slivered almonds

Preheat the oven to 350°. Grease and lightly flour two large cookie sheets.

Combine the flour, sugar, baking powder, and salt in a large bowl.

In a separate bowl, whisk together the eggs, vanilla, and one tablespoon of water. Pour this mixture into the flour mixture. Using a sturdy spoon or a mixer, mix until well incorporated. The dough will be very stiff.

Divide the dough into 2 parts. Mix the cocoa into 1 part and the instant coffee into the other. You may need to use your hands. Add the almonds to the chocolate dough, mixing well.

Break each piece of dough in half. Use your hands to roll the 4 pieces into logs. Place a coffee-flavored log next to a chocolate log. Roll the 2 together firmly until the combined log is about 11 inches long and 4 inches wide. Press down on top of the log to flatten it, so that it spreads out to about 6 inches wide. Combine the other coffee log and chocolate log in the same way.

Place the 2 large logs on the cookie sheets and bake for 35–40 minutes, until golden and firm. They will spread out during the baking.

Cool the loaves on a baking rack, then use a serrated knife to cut each loaf at an angle into ³/₄-inch-thick slices. Return the slices to the cookie sheets, laying them flat. Bake for 10–15 minutes more at the same temperature to dry the biscotti. Turn the slices over halfway through the baking time.

Cool the biscotti on wire racks and allow to finish drying. Store in an airtight container.

Makes about 2 dozen large biscotti.

Biscotti, an Italian tradition, are usually served as a dunking treat with milk, coffee, or espresso. By baking the dough twice, you assure that the biscotti will be very dry and hard, but also that they will last for a long time if stored in an airtight container. Perhaps this frugal part of the Italian nature helped Italian immigrants to survive. These wonderful indestructible desserts are a terrific addition to care packages—they will arrive at their destination looking just as delicious as they did when they came out of the oven.

RASPBERRY-RHUBARB SORBET

2 tablespoons raspberry liqueur

1 pint fresh raspberries, rinsed and drained

1/2 cup orange juice

1 cup sugar

2 tablespoons freshly squeezed lemon juice

4 cups chopped rhubarb—cut the stalks into 1/2-inch pieces

1/4 cup water

Sprinkle the liqueur over the raspberries and set aside.

Combine the orange juice, sugar, lemon juice, rhubarb, and water in a medium-sized saucepan. Bring the mixture to a boil over high heat. Reduce the heat to low and stir continuously until the rhubarb is tender, about 15–20 minutes.

Purée the rhubarb mixture in a food processor until smooth. Pour into a bowl.

Add the raspberries and liqueur to the processor and purée them. Fold the raspberry purée into the rhubarb mixture and allow to cool. Scoop into an ice cream maker and freeze according to the manufacturer's instructions.

Remove the sorbet from the ice cream maker and pack it into a sealable container. Cover and freeze for at least 4 hours.

Serves 8–12.

Living in the South, where fresh, ripe raspberries are not abundant, I was forced to be berry stingy. When I returned home, I welcomed the sight of Montana's overgrown raspberry bushes with their dewy, berry-laden branches. In Montana, we've been known to pick more than a gallon of raspberries a day—the berries practically fall from the branches into our buckets.

The Chocolate Mocha Biscotti (page 126) is a perfect pairing with this sorbet.

PECAN BIZCOCHITOS

1 cup lard or butter at room temperature

$^1/_2$ cup granulated sugar

$^1/_8$ cup anise liqueur or $^1/_2$ teaspoon anise extract with $^1/_8$ cup apple juice

3 egg yolks

$1^1/_2$ teaspoons baking powder

3 cups unbleached white flour

$^1/_2$ cup coarsely chopped pecans

2 teaspoons ground cinnamon combined with 2 tablespoons sugar

non-stick cooking spray

Preheat the oven to 350°. Coat 2 baking sheets with non-stick spray.

Using an electric mixer, cream together the lard or butter and the sugar until fluffy. Add the anise liqueur and egg yolks and beat until well combined. Finally, add the baking powder, flour, and pecans. Mix just until the flour is incorporated.

Roll tablespoonfuls of dough in your hands and place them on the cookie sheets. Dip the bottom of a glass in cinnamon sugar and press it on top of the cookies to flatten them into $^1/_4$-inch circles.

Bake for 8–10 minutes or until lightly browned. Let cool on racks and store in an airtight container.

Makes 2–3 dozen bizcochitos

Bizcochitos were actually voted the state cookie by New Mexico's state legislature. It's rare to find a café or coffee shop in New Mexico that doesn't serve bizcochitos. You'll find them in every imaginable shape, but the most traditional shape is the fleur-de-lys.

Bizcochitos are typically prepared with lard and whole aniseeds. I prefer them made with butter and with ground aniseed. Ground, they distribute throughout the cookies better.

I find the use of butter in bizcochitos gives them a smoother and warmer flavor.

I'm also aware that bizcochitos don't usually have nuts in them. So, to make a more nearly authentic New Mexican state cookie, don't forget to use pecans from the massive pecan orchards south of Mesilla, New Mexico. Pecans are not just grown in the deep South. Mesilla's 3,600-acre orchard is the second largest in the world.

HUCKLEBERRY BREAD PUDDING

    6 cups 1-inch French bread cubes
    1 quart milk
    4 eggs
1 1/2 cups sugar
    2 teaspoons vanilla extract
    1 cup huckleberries, fresh, frozen, or canned
    3 tablespoons butter, melted
  1/2 teaspoon cinnamon
    3 tablespoons brandy or bourbon

Preheat the oven to 350°. Lightly grease a casserole dish or baking pan.

Fill a large mixing bowl with bread cubes.

In a separate bowl, combine the remaining ingredients. Pour this mixture over the bread cubes. Stir to coat the bread well. Let sit for about 10 minutes so the liquid can soak into the bread. Stir again and pour into the prepared baking dish.

Cover the dish with foil or a lid and bake for about 40 minutes. Uncover and bake an additional 5–10 minutes or until firm and not runny in the center.

Let the pudding cool partially, then spoon it into dessert bowls. Serve warm, topped with ice cream, milk, whipped cream, or hard sauce.

Serves 8–10.

The Izaak Walton Inn in Essex, Montana, is on the southern border of Glacier National Park, right in the heart of huckleberry country. The inn's manager will long remember a less-than-laudatory comment he once made about huckleberries to a big city reporter. The reporter wrote an article about the historic train station-turned inn, and the huckleberry comment is the most-quoted sentence in the entire article. The manager was discussing the superior culinary qualities of his inn's restaurant when the reporter asked him point-blank whether or not he liked the huckleberry-sauced chicken entrée on the menu. His honest answer was that he couldn't stand that particular entrée. Locals and visitors alike were amazed that anyone could have something bad to say about any dish smothered in the much-revered huckleberry. I rejoiced, figuring that meant at least one less individual to compete with me out there in the huckleberry patch.

FLATHEAD CHERRY FUDGE TORTE

2 cups crumbled pecan shortbread cookies

1/4 cup Irish Cream, Kahlua, or preferred liqueur

1 1/2 cups pecan or walnut halves

8 ounces semisweet or bittersweet chocolate

5 ounces milk chocolate

2 eggs at room temperature

2 tablespoons sugar

2 sticks (1/2 pound) butter, melted

1/2 cup dried cherries

Line the bottom of an 8-inch round cake pan with a circle of waxed paper.

In a mixing bowl, combine the liqueur with the cookie crumbs, tossing until the crumbs are evenly moistened.

Set aside 10 nut halves for decoration. Coarsely chop the remaining nuts and add them to the cookie mixture.

Break all the chocolate pieces into 1-inch cubes and put them in a double boiler over medium heat. Stir until melted—about 5 minutes. Or you can microwave the chocolate on high for 1–1 1/2 minutes, stirring every 30 seconds until it is completely melted.

In a separate bowl, beat the eggs and sugar until the sugar dissolves, about 2 minutes. Drizzle the melted butter into the sugar-egg mixture, beating with a whisk or a wooden spoon until smooth. Add this mixture to the melted chocolate, beating until smooth again. Finally, stir the soaked cookie crumbs and dried cherries into the chocolate until well incorporated.

Scrape the batter into the lined pan. Arrange the reserved nut halves around the top edge of the torte. Refrigerate uncovered for 1 1/2–2 hours, or until firm.

Loosen the torte from the sides of the pan with a blunt knife, invert on an extra plate, and peel the wax paper from the bottom. Turn the torte right side up again on a serving platter. The torte will only be about 1 1/2 inches high. Slice in thin wedges.

Serves 15–20.

When I did a Rocky Mountain gourmet cooking segment on KRTV in Great Falls, Montana, this recipe drew the greatest number of viewer requests for printed copies. If I'd have called it something more prosaic like "No-Bake Cake," all gourmands within earshot of the program might well have turned their noses up at the less-than-elegant-sounding name. The truth is that, essentially, this is a no-bake cake. On the other hand, it is also one of the most refined-looking creations I make, and the use of high-quality bulk chocolate assures an especially smooth and complicated-tasting palate pleaser. I've used good chocolate chips in a pinch. But I detect a definite difference when I purchase gourmet-quality Swiss chocolate. It's really the only way to get a true bittersweet chocolate, which transforms the torte into a cherry-rich dessert with deep coffee undertones. Use plump, moist dried cherries that are more tart than sweet, like those picked in the lakeside orchards of Montana's Flathead Valley.

SPICED NATIVE AMERICAN BLUE CORN PUDDING

$1/2$ cup blue cornmeal

$1/2$ cup water

1 quart scalded milk

$1/2$ cup molasses

$1/4$ cup sugar

2 teaspoons ground ginger

$1/2$ teaspoon cinnamon

$1/4$ teaspoon nutmeg

$3/4$ teaspoon salt

1 cup cold milk

Preheat the oven to 300°. Grease a 9 x 13-inch baking dish.

Combine the cornmeal and water. Stir this mixture into the scalded milk. Add the molasses, sugar, spices, and salt, mixing well.

Pour the pudding into the prepared baking dish and bake for 25 minutes.

Add the cold milk without stirring and bake for 3 hours longer.

Serves 6–8.

Atole is the name for a corn gruel that was a staple in the diets of early Hispanic and Native American families. The dessert version of this gruel can be sweetened in a variety of ways: with honey, brown sugar, granulated sugar, or molasses. This very simple recipe is for blue corn pudding, but you can substitute white or yellow cornmeal for the blue.

I once had blue corn pudding at a restaurant in Santa Fe, New Mexico. The restaurant, situated in a historic building near the plaza, served its blue corn pudding garnished with pine nuts, raisins, and Pine Nut Brittle (page 138). To dress up this peasant dessert for guests, drizzle a creative-looking swirl of raspberry or blueberry purée across each serving, drop a few pine nuts on top, and place an artfully broken shard of Pine Nut Brittle or a sugar cookie on the side.

APPLE TART TATIN

1 tablespoon butter
1 cup sugar
4 apples (any variety)
2 sheets puff pastry

Preheat the oven to 375°. Butter a cast iron skillet well.

Cut the puff pastry to size of the pan, poke it in several places with a fork, and set it aside.

Pour the sugar into the skillet, coat the bottom and sides, and dump out the excess.

Slice the apples into thin ($1/4$-inch) slices. Layer the slices in a tight pinwheel circle over the sugar in the pan. Place the pastry on top.

Put the skillet on the stovetop over medium-high heat and cook the tart until the sugar turns caramel-colored. Transfer the skillet to the oven and bake for about 15 minutes or until the puff pastry is browned. Turn upside down onto a serving dish.

Serves 4.

Each course of the following menu includes ingredients and a style of cooking from a different culture: Asian, Italian, Jamaican, New Mexican. When I am trying to create a meal with an interesting array of textures, colors, and flavors, I sometimes mix foods from different cultures. It seems the best way to ensure that none of the courses overlap in flavors.

Suggested Menu:

- Trout in Lemon Broth with Peas (page 38)
- Walnut, Garlic, and Sun-dried Tomato Foccacia (page 159)
- Jerk-Style Grilled Pheasant (page 95)
- Steamed Carrots and Zucchini with Chipotle Chili Butter (page 63)
- Apple Tart Tatin

FINNISH GOLDEN RAISIN-ALMOND CAKE

1¼ cups unbleached flour
1 teaspoon cinnamon
1 teaspoon cardamom
¼ teaspoon cloves
¼ teaspoon allspice
1 teaspoon baking powder
½ teaspoon baking soda
½ teaspoon salt
2 eggs
¾ cup packed brown sugar
1 teaspoon vanilla
⅓ cup butter, melted

1 cup sour cream
⅓ cup golden raisins
½ cup slivered almonds

Preheat the oven to 350°. Grease an 8-inch fluted tube pan.

Combine the flour, spices, baking powder, baking soda, and salt in a mixing bowl. Set aside.

Using an electric mixer on medium-high speed, beat the eggs, brown sugar, and vanilla together for 3 minutes or until the mixture is thick. Add the melted butter and mix until it is incorporated. Alternately add the flour mixture and the sour cream, beating on low speed after each addition until combined.

Stir in the golden raisins and almonds and pour the batter into the prepared pan. Bake for 45–55 minutes or until a cake tester inserted in the center comes out clean.

Cool the cake for 10 minutes on a wire rack then invert the pan to remove the cake. Serve plain or with a frosting made by mixing an additional cup of sour cream with ¼ cup powdered sugar and ¼ teaspoon vanilla (mix until smooth).

Serves 8–12.

Telluride, Colorado, had a thriving Finnish community in its early days. This settlement of Finnish immigrants helped build and work Telluride's mines. The area the Finn's settled became known as Finn Town, and it had several boarding houses that served Finnish dried-fuit cakes similar to this traditional dessert.

DRIED CHERRY- AND CHOCOLATE - STUDDED GINGERBREAD CAKE

½ cup shortening

½ cup sugar

2 eggs

1 cup molasses

1½ cups unbleached white flour

1 cup whole wheat flour

1½ teaspoons baking soda

1½ teaspoons ground ginger

1 teaspoon ground cinnamon

½ teaspoon ground cloves

½ teaspoon salt

1 cup hot water

½ cup dried cherries

½ cup dark chocolate chips

non-stick cooking spray

Preheat the oven to 350°. Spray 9 x 13-inch cake pan with non-stick cooking spray.

Using an electric mixer, cream together the shortening and sugar. Add the eggs and molasses and mix until well incorporated. Add the dry ingredients and the hot water. Beat until smooth.

Fold in the cherries and chocolate chips by hand. Spoon the batter into the greased pan. Bake for 30–35 minutes or until your fingertip pressed into the top of the cake does not leave an indentation.

Serve with whipped cream or frost with butter cream or cream cheese frosting.

Serves 8–12.

I'll start out by admitting that in a pinch, when I don't have time to be a gourmet, I forgo the homemade gingerbread recipe and use a boxed gingerbread cake mix, adding the dried cherries and chocolate chips. If you don't have dried cherries and don't feel like going to the store, try this cake with golden raisins. If you have a favorite lemon curd recipe, spread that on top of a slice of gingerbread cake instead of whipped cream or frosting. Cooking is parallel to living in my book, and requires the same relaxed attitude to make things turn out right. Be flexible.

GERMAN SOUR CREAM PASTRY TWISTS

3$\frac{1}{2}$ cups flour

1 teaspoon salt

1 cup shortening

1 package active dry yeast

$\frac{1}{4}$ cup very warm water (115°)

$\frac{3}{4}$ cup real sour cream

1 egg and 2 egg yolks, beaten lightly

1 teaspoon vanilla

1 cup sugar

Combine the flour and salt in a mixing bowl. Cut in the shortening with a pastry knife.

Dissolve the yeast in the water. Stir the dissolved yeast into the flour mixture. Add the sour cream, eggs, and vanilla and mix well.

Cover the dough with a damp cloth and refrigerate for 2 hours.

Preheat the oven to 375°. Grease 2 baking sheets.

Roll half the dough on a sugar-covered board into an 8 x 16-inch rectangle. Fold the ends toward center, overlapping them. Sprinkle the top surface with sugar. Roll the dough out to the same size (8 x 16 inches) again, fold it, and sugar it. Repeat the procedure a third time.

After sugaring the dough the third time, roll it out to $\frac{1}{4}$-inch thickness. Cut it into 1 x 4-inch strips. Twist the ends of each strip in opposite directions, then shape the twists into horseshoes on the prepared baking sheet.

Repeat the entire procedure with the other half of the dough.

Bake for 15 minutes at 375°, until barely golden on the bottom.

Makes 3–4 dozen.

This recipe came to me via my grandmother. I've come across similar recipes in church cookbooks with other ethnicities tied to them. I'm just fascinated by how simple these pastry twists are to make and how flaky and puff pastry-like they turn out. These twists are one of the most elegant desserts I make, especially when served with a bowl of fresh berries topped with a tablespoon of port wine.

MUSHER'S CREAM CHEESE SHORTBREAD COOKIES

1 cup butter

6 ounces cream cheese

1 cup sugar

1 teaspoon vanilla

$^1/_2$ teaspoon salt

1 egg, slightly beaten

2 tablespoons milk

2 cups flour

$^3/_4$ cup chopped cashews, peanuts, pecans,
   or walnuts

Preheat the oven to 350°.

Using an electric mixer, cream together the butter, cream cheese, sugar, vanilla, salt, and egg until everything is well incorporated. Add the milk, flour, and nuts and mix well.

Drop the dough by heaping tablespoonfuls onto an ungreased baking sheet. Bake for 15–17 minutes, until firm.

Makes 4$^1/_2$ dozen cookies.

Judy Johnson raises and shows Siberian sled dogs. She shares a kennel in Elliston, Montana, with musher Dave Torgerson. She also handles Torgerson's sled dogs, which are mostly Alaskan-Husky mixes.

More than one Montana musher packs Johnson's shortbread cookies in the sled to snack on during long training runs and races. "They're awesome," says Torgerson. "They're nothing but butter and sugar and that's great for getting you down the trail. We depend on the fat to help keep us warm and the sugar for energy. They don't freeze solid, so you can eat them without breaking your teeth." The cookies are more than just butter and sugar, as the recipe shows, but Torgerson knows what's important in a musher's race diet and Johnson's cookies are on the top of his list.

CARDAMOM-PORT FLAN

¹/₂ cup water

1¹/₂ cups sugar

1 cup tawney port

1¹/₃ cup cream or half-and-half

4 large eggs

¹/₄ teaspoon Mexican vanilla

¹/₄ teaspoon salt

¹/₄ teaspoon cardamom

fresh berries for garnish

Preheat the oven to 350°.

In a small saucepan over medium-high heat, bring the water and 1 cup of the sugar to a boil, stirring for the first 3 minutes. Brush down the sides of the pan with a pastry brush dipped in water to prevent sugar crystals from forming. Boil the syrup until it is a deep golden-brown color, then divide it among 6 ¹/₂-cup custard cups.

In a medium-sized saucepan, boil the port until it's reduced to ¹/₂ cup; this should take about 10 minutes. Remove the port from the heat and add the remaining ¹/₂ cup sugar. Stir until the sugar dissolves. Whisk in the cream or half-and-half, eggs, vanilla, salt, and cardamom.

Pour the custard mixture into the caramel-lined cups, dividing it evenly among the 6. Place the cups in a baking pan. Add hot water to the baking pan to reach halfway up the sides of the cups.

Bake for about 40 minutes, until a knife inserted into the center of a cup comes out clean. Cool the flans in the refrigerator overnight .

Invert the flans on dessert plates to serve. Top with fresh berries for garnish, and serve with Pine Nut Brittle (page 138).

Makes 6 flans.

A little place called the Center Café in Moab, Utah, serves a port flan. Though my recipe is laced with the exotic flavor of cardamom, it was inspired by the dish at Moab's culinary hotspot.

Reducing the fortified wine creates such an intensity of port flavor that anyone who tastes it in the flan is surprised, and usually comes out with something like, "Oh my gosh, what's in this stuff?!" I love that kind of reaction to my cooking. I learned to cook with port at the Messina Hof Winery in Bryan, Texas. They produced a dark, cherry-colored version that the wine-maker's grandfather used to make in the bathtub of his New York City apartment.

This port flan is quite simple. It also provides good nourishment for someone who is just getting back to solid foods following a surgery or illness.

PINE NUT BRITTLE

2 cups pine nuts
2½ cups granulated sugar

Preheat the oven to 300°.

Spread the pine nuts on a baking sheet. Toast them in the oven for about 15 minutes or until they begin to turn golden.

Line another baking sheet with foil.

Pour the sugar into a frying pan. Cook it over medium heat, stirring constantly until it melts—about 8–10 minutes. Reduce the heat and continue to stir until the sugar turns an amber color, about 2–5 minutes longer.

Quickly, before the sugar sets, mix in the roasted pine nuts and pour the mixture onto the foil-lined baking sheet. Spread it into a thin layer and let cool for at least 25 minutes.

Peel the foil from the brittle and break it into pieces. Store in an airtight container.

The Santa Clara Pueblo Indians in New Mexico say pinyon trees are the oldest living trees. They grow at elevations between 4,000 and 7,000 feet and are short and squatty in stature. Pine nuts are harvested from the trees in late fall and early winter. They are usually roasted in a basket with live coals; the roasters shake the baskets until the earthy scent of the seeds wafts out. While still warm, the nuts are rolled between moist towels with a rolling pin to crack their shells, then are picked from the towels to be stored.

Native tribes with access to pinyon trees used the pine nuts to make a gruel for babies. The nuts are quite rich in protein and fat—every pound of nuts contains 3,000 calories. The ground nutmeal is so oily that some individuals rub it into their shoes to waterproof them. Pueblo Indians, as well as other native tribes, also ground pine nuts to make flat, high-energy cakes.

While pine nuts have become a somewhat trendy culinary ingredient, they have always been a staple for some groups of people, including Italians and other Mediterranean families who harvest the same nuts from trees in their region.

Serve this brittle with Cardamom-Port Flan (page 137).

CRANBERRY- AND WALNUT-STUFFED APPLE DUMPLINGS IN WHISKEY SYRUP

Syrup:
1/2 teaspoon vanilla
6 tablespoons whiskey
1 1/2 cups apple juice
1/2 cup honey
1/2 teaspoon ground ginger
1/8 teaspoon ground nutmeg
3/4 teaspoon ground cinnamon

Stuffing:
4 tablespoons chopped walnuts
1/4 cup dried cranberries
4 tablespoons brown sugar

dough for 1 double-crust pie
4 apples, peeled and cored whole
4 tablespoons butter
vanilla ice cream

Preheat the oven to 350°.

To make the syrup, combine the vanilla, whiskey, apple juice, honey, 1/4 teaspoon of the ginger, all the nutmeg, and 1/2 teaspoon of the cinnamon in a small saucepan. Bring the mixture to a boil over medium heat. Reduce the heat and simmer on low for about 8 minutes. Remove from the heat and set aside.

In a small bowl, combine the ingredients for the stuffing: the remaining 1/4 teaspoon of ginger and 1/4 teaspoon of cinnamon, the walnuts, the cranberries, and the brown sugar. Set aside.

To start the dumplings, divide the pie dough into 4 balls. Roll each ball into a round that is 5–6 inches in diameter. Cut 3 or 4 notches around the edges of each circle; the notches should reach halfway into the middle of the circle. Set an apple in the center of each circle and wrap the dough up around it, using the notches to help fold one section of dough over the other without too much bulk. Press the seams firmly to seal. Leave a large opening at the top.

Fill the center of each apple with the walnut-cranberry stuffing, dividing the stuffing evenly among the 4 apples. Arrange the apples in a deep baking pan. Dot the top of each apple with 1 tablespoon of butter. Pour a tablespoon of the whiskey syrup in the top of each apple over the stuffing. Pour the rest of the syrup around the base of the apples.

Bake for about 30 minutes, until the apples are tender when tested with a knife. Serve the apples warm, topped with syrup from the bottom of the pan and vanilla ice cream.

Serves 4.

I'd never actually tasted an apple dumpling until my friend Annie Beaver made them for me and several other guests, using Annie's grandmother's recipe. Annie wrapped each apple up like a package in rolled-out pie dough. Cutting the notches from the dough rounds is Annie's invention for dealing with the heavy mass of dough that accumulates around each apple. The dough fits more snugly this way. Of course, if you like all that dough, don't cut the notches.

I adjusted Annie's recipe by adding the fruit-nut stuffing and the whiskey syrup; I also added a bit of whole wheat flour to my pie crust, for a nutty taste.

ROCKY TRIPLE NUT CHEESECAKE

Crust:

  1 cup all-purpose flour

  ¼ cup coarsely ground almonds

  ¼ cup sugar

  ⅓ cup butter, melted

  1 tablespoon grated lemon zest

Filling:

  5 8-ounce packages cream cheese

1½ cups sugar

  1 tablespoon lemon zest

  5 eggs

  ¼ cup cornstarch

juice of 1 lemon

  1 pint sour cream

  1 tablespoon vanilla extract

  ½ cup roasted, chopped hazelnuts

  ½ cup roasted, chopped pecans

  ½ cup brown sugar

  ¼ cup butter

  ¼ cup whipping cream

Preheat the oven to 300°. Grease a 10-inch springform pan.

Combine the crust ingredients in a mixing bowl. Press the crust into a thin layer covering the sides and bottom of the prepared pan. Bake for about 8 minutes to set. Remove from the oven and allow to cool.

To make the filling: Using an electric mixer, beat the cream cheese, sugar, and lemon zest in a large bowl until fluffy. Add the eggs, 1 at a time while mixing. Add the cornstarch and beat well to incorporate. Mix in the lemon juice, sour cream, and vanilla.

Pour the filling over the cooled crust. Bake for 40 minutes in the 300° oven.

While the cheesecake is baking, combine the nuts, brown sugar, butter, and whipping cream in a saucepan over medium heat. Bring to a boil and cook for 3–5 minutes, until the sugar dissolves and the sauce thickens.

After the cheesecake has baked for 40 minutes, pour the sauce over its center; try to prevent any sauce from seeping down the sides. Return the cheesecake to the oven and bake for an additional 20 minutes.

Turn the oven off and leave the oven door ajar, allowing the cheesecake to cool completely in the oven. Refrigerate for at least 6 hours before serving.

Serves 8–12.

My favorite dessert wine with this cheesecake is a fortified Late Harvest Riesling. The way this wine is produced shows that good things do come to those who wait. The grapes are allowed to become almost like raisins on the vine. Then, just as the first frost sets in, they are picked—but with the utmost care, because the yield is about a fourth of what most grape crops produce.

Low
Fat

Merlot- and Honey-Poached Pears with Cinnamon Ricotta

    4 red d'Anjou or Bosc pears, peeled
    2 cups Merlot wine—or Cabernet if preferred
  3/4 cup honey
    2 tablespoons lemon juice
    1 cinnamon stick
1 1/3 cups light or nonfat ricotta cheese
  1/2 teaspoon vanilla
  1/4 teaspoon ground cinnamon

       toasted coconut (toast in a 350° oven until
         golden, about 8 minutes) for garnish

Cut the pears in half lengthwise and remove the cores.

In a large saucepan over medium heat, bring the wine, 1/2 cup of the honey, the lemon juice, and the cinnamon stick to a boil. Add the pears, reduce the heat, and simmer, covered, for about 12–15 minutes, until the pears are tender. Using a slotted spoon, remove the pears to a bowl.

Continue to simmer the sauce until it has reduced to about 3/4 cup. Discard the cinnamon stick. Cool the sauce and the pears in the refrigerator.

Fold the ricotta, the remaining 1/4 cup of honey, the vanilla, and the ground cinnamon together in a bowl.

Divide the reduced merlot sauce among 4 shallow bowls. Lay 2 pear halves in each puddle of sauce. Spoon the sweetened ricotta into the hollows of the pears, using about 1/3 cup of the filling per plate. Garnish with toasted coconut.

Serves 4.

Lowfat and nonfat cheese products clearly don't have that creamy texture we so adore, but they fit well into a recipe like this, in which "light" cheese is paired with the complex flavors of fruit poached in a slightly peppery wine. Mixing the honey into the cheese in this recipe also smooths the grainier texture of the lowfat or nonfat ricotta.

In other recipes, I've successfully substituted for fatty cheeses by combining several lowfat dairy products—using a mixture of sour cream, cream cheese, and ricotta or cottage cheese—to create a creamier texture. No, the lowfat alternatives don't taste the same as the "real thing," but if you want to enjoy a dessert while sticking to a heart-healthy eating plan, lowfat cheese products can give you valuable options.

HUCKLEBERRY BITTERSWEET CHOCOLATE TRUFFLES

12 ounces bittersweet chocolate, broken into small pieces

¼ cup butter

¾ cup heavy cream

½ cup huckleberry jam

3 tablespoons cognac or brandy

cocoa powder

8 ounces bittersweet chocolate for hand dipping (optional)

In a double boiler over low heat, melt the chocolate and butter together, stirring frequently. When both have melted, remove from the heat and whisk gently to combine well.

Scald the cream. Add it gradually to the chocolate mixture, stirring constantly with a wire whisk. Add the huckleberry jam and cognac. Cover and chill until firm, from 4 hours to overnight.

Line a baking sheet with wax paper. Using a melon ball scoop or a rounded tablespoon, scoop out walnut-sized truffles and roll them quickly into balls between cocoa-powder-dusted palms. Place the truffles on the lined baking sheet and refrigerate until firm.

Roll the chilled truffles in more cocoa powder or cover them in melted chocolate. To do the latter, melt 8 ounces of bittersweet chocolate in a double boiler over low heat. Drop the truffles into the melted chocolate, remove them with your fingers, and place them back on the lined baking sheet to harden.

Makes 12–15 truffles.

This truffle recipe can be used as a basic starting point for all kinds of wonderful treats. Add any liqueur and any fruit jam or purée to the chocolate cream filling and you've got yourself a new truffle. One year I made about five different kinds of truffles for Christmas presents. I rolled them in a variety of toppings—cocoa; nuts; white, dark, and milk chocolate—and I packaged them in decorated boxes.

MEXICAN CHOCOLATE MOCHA FONDUE

Fondue:

16 ounces Mexican or dark chocolate

 1 cup heavy cream

 ½ cup sweetened condensed milk

 ¼ cup black coffee

 1 teaspoon Mexican or other good quality vanilla extract

 ½ teaspoon cinnamon

 6 tablespoons Kahlua

Dippers:

fresh fruits—strawberries; apple, kiwi, and pineapple chunks; orange slices

dried fruits

cubes of pound cake

nuts

cookies

In a double boiler over low-medium heat, combine all the fondue ingredients except the Kahlua. Stir until everything is melted and smooth. Remove from the heat and stir in the Kahlua.

Pour the sauce into a fondue pot or chafing dish. Set the dish in the center of the table and serve with your choice of dippers, along with coffee and liqueurs.

Serves 6–8.

For some reason, fondue seems to have gone out of fashion. There must be hundreds of thousands of fondue pots tucked away on the tops of garage shelves throughout the country. On a recent trip to a pawn shop, I had my pick of a variety of styles, some electric, some with candles, others set up for sterno. Whichever method you prefer, I'd encourage a revival of the 1970s-era fondue parties: vegetables and meat dipped in tempura batter and deep-fat fried; cubes of bread doused in cheesy-beer sauce; and fruits, cake, and nuts scooped into a rich pot of chocolate. Nothing seems more appropriate in an alpine setting than a fondue pot in the center of a table that's surrounded by friends.

There must have been a reason fondue parties were such a rage. I believe it was because they were so much fun and because they were so simple for the cook to prepare.

BREADS

Tassajara Bread

Navajo Fry Bread Mulato

Savory Butternut Squash Fritters

Apricot–Almond Scones

Homemade Whole Grain Baking Mix

Carrot–Banana Bran Muffins

Beer Bread with Parmesan and Basil

Sweet Potato Biscuits

Sourdough Starter

Sourdough Basque Sheepherder's Bread

Blue Corn Muffins with Chilies

Whole Wheat–Red Pepper Tortillas

Mu Shu Wrappers

Walnut, Garlic, and Sun-dried Tomato Foccacia

Vegetable–Herb Dumplings

Cheddar Biscuits with Thyme and Sage

Dried Cranberry–Oat Soda Bread

Swedish Rye Limpa with Aniseed and Currants

Huckleberry Swirl Bread

Sage Popovers

Polenta–Pumpkin Madeleines with Thyme

Savory Chocolate and Red Chili Breadsticks

TASSAJARA BREAD

½ cup whole milk

½ cup honey

4 tablespoons molasses

1 cup whole wheat flour

½ cup rolled oats

½ cup cracked millet

½ cup unbleached white flour

1 teaspoon salt

1 tablespoon baking powder

1 tablespoon sesame seeds

1 tablespoon poppy seeds

1 tablespoon sunflower seeds

1 cup lowfat buttermilk

2 eggs

¼ cup canola oil

Preheat oven to 400 °. Grease a loaf pan.

Heat the whole milk, honey, and molasses in a small saucepan over medium heat until well blended. Remove from heat and set aside.

Combine all dry ingredients in a mixing bowl and stir well.

Beat the buttermilk, eggs, and oil into the sweetened milk. Fold the wet mixture into the dry ingredients until just blended.

Spoon the batter into the greased loaf pan. Bake for 50–60 minutes, until golden; test for doneness by touching the top of the loaf—your finger should leave no imprint. Cool in the pan for 10 minutes, then turn the loaf out onto a cooling rack.

Makes 1 loaf.

The Tassajara Bread Book was written by Edward Espe Brown for the Zen Mountain Center in the Tassajara Valley near Monterey, California, back in the 1970s and is still a "hippie classic." The bread recipe above was inspired by the Tassajara book's emphasis on baking with whole grains and combining various grains for optimum nutrients, flavor, and texture.

The Tassajara Bread Book was the first cookbook I ever bought for myself, purchased when I was a University of Montana freshman sick of eating every meal at the university food service. I still own that book—plus about a million other cookbooks—a self-described obsession.

NAVAJO FRY BREAD MULATO

4 tablespoons sugar

$^1/_2$ cup whole milk

$^1/_4$ cup water

$^1/_4$ cup canola oil

1 teaspoon salt

2 tablespoons hand-crushed mulato chilies

1 package active dry yeast

2 cups all-purpose flour

3 cups whole wheat flour

2 eggs

vegetable oil in deep fat fryer
    (to at a least 3-inch depth)

Combine the sugar, milk, water, oil, salt, and chilies in a saucepan and heat until very warm (120°–130°) over low-medium heat.

In a mixing bowl, stir the yeast into 1$^1/_2$ cups of the all-purpose flour. Whisk the liquid and the eggs into the mixing bowl with the flour and yeast and beat for 2–3 minutes until smooth.

Using a large mixing spoon, mix all the whole wheat flour and as much of the additional all-purpose flour as you can into this batter. Drop the resulting dough onto a floured board and knead in enough flour to make it stiff. Continue kneading for about 7 more minutes, until the dough becomes smooth and elastic.

Grease the mixing bowl. Put the dough inside it, cover, and let rise in a warm place for 30 minutes. Then, punch it down and turn it onto floured board. Cover and let rise another 15 minutes.

Using a floured rolling pin, roll the dough to a $^1/_4$-inch thickness and cut into 3 x 4-inch rectangles.

Heat the cooking oil to 370° in a deep fryer or electric fry pan. Carefully drop 2 pieces of dough at a time into the hot oil and fry until golden, about 2 minutes. Drain on paper towels. Serve warm with honey or green chili salsa, depending on whether the occasion, meal, or preference calls for sweet or savory flavors.

Makes about 15 rectangles.

The mulato chili, almost red-black in color with a rich smoky flavor, is the dried form of the poblano chili. To crumble the mulatos for this bread, you will need to rub them between your hands.

Almost any Navajo Indian Reservation, New Mexican Pueblo, or Northern Rockies Native American tribe will have a way of making fry bread that they call their own. It is frequenlty served drizzled with honey. I've also enjoyed fry bread as a base for what is called an Indian Taco, topped with spicy beef, lettuce, tomatoes, and salsa.

SAVORY BUTTERNUT SQUASH FRITTERS

vegetable oil in deep fat fryer
  (to at least a 3-inch depth)
1 cup unbleached white flour
¼ cup cornmeal
1 teaspoon baking powder
½ cup milk
1 tablespoon brown sugar
2 eggs
½ cup mashed, pre-baked butternut squash
1 teaspoon canola oil
1 teaspoon salt
2 tablespoons finely minced onion

½ teaspoon dried thyme or
  1 teaspoon fresh thyme leaves
¼ teaspoon red pepper flakes

Preheat the oil to 370° in a deep fryer or electric skillet.

Combine the flour, cornmeal, and baking powder in a mixing bowl. Add all the remaining ingredients and stir until just moistened.

Drop tablespoons full into the hot oil and fry for 3–5 minutes, until brown on the surface and done in the middle. You may need to test the first one to determine the amount of time this takes. Drain the fritters on paper towels and serve immediately. Batter may be kept refrigerated for up to 6 hours before use.

Makes about 16 fritters.

Just a few steps from the historic plaza in Santa Fe, New Mexico, you'll find the elegant Inn of the Anasazi. The inn's rooms are filled with pure Santa Fe charm—kiva fireplaces, dark Spanish antiques, and four-poster beds. The meals served at the inn are exquisite. I had duck-filled blue corn tamales smothered in apricot sauce that were earthy and sweet. I also had my first real fritters there. I think they were studded with bits of Ancho chili and nutmeg. They were crisp, light, and practically void of any greasy residue. I've been fascinated with fritters, or Hush Puppies—if that's what you grew up calling these nuggets of deep-fat-fried batter—ever since.

The mashed squash in this recipe creates a tender, moist fritter with a hint of sweetness to comfort the tongue when confronted with a fiery meal of New Mexican chilies.

APRICOT-ALMOND SCONES

2 cups all-purpose flour

1/3 cup sugar

1 1/2 teaspoons baking powder

3/4 teaspoon salt

4 tablespoons butter

1 cup lowfat buttermilk

1 egg

4 tablespoons apricot jam

1/4 cup minced dried apricots

1/4 cup almonds, finely slivered

1 teaspoon finely grated fresh lemon zest

Preheat the oven to 425°. Grease a large baking sheet.

Combine the flour, sugar, baking powder, and salt in a large mixing bowl. Cut the butter into the dry ingredients with a pastry knife until the mixture resembles coarse pebbles. Add the remaining ingredients, stirring to combine.

Drop the dough in 3-tablespoon-sized mounds onto the baking sheet. Bake for about 15 minutes, until golden.

Makes 12–16 scones.

A family vacation to Banff National Park in the Canadian Rockies, and to the historic Banff Springs Hotel in particular, provided my first encounter with the British tradition of high tea. As a youngster, I noticed the china plates decorated with a heady variety of finger-foods including cookies, tiny sandwiches, and what I thought were biscuits, which turned out to be currant scones. The butter in the small bowls was actually clotted cream.

A lot of scones are a bit dry and crumbly for my taste, but this recipe does a good job of making sure the scone doesn't fall apart in your hand as it approaches your mouth. I also replaced the traditional currants with apricots, and threw in some almonds for a bit of crunch.

HOMEMADE WHOLE GRAIN BAKING MIX

1½ cups all-purpose flour

2½ cups whole wheat flour

2 tablespoons sugar

½ cup old-fashioned oats

⅔ cup dry nonfat milk powder

½ cup cornmeal

¾ teaspoon salt

2 tablespoons baking powder

1 cup shortening

Combine all the dry ingredients in a large mixing bowl. Cut the shortening into the dry ingredients with a pastry knife until the mixture resembles tiny pebbles.

Keep the mix in a sealed container in the refrigerator for best freshness. A cool, dry cupboard will also work if the seal is airtight.

To use: For biscuits, add enough water to make a stiff dough, about ⅓–½ cup for every cup of dry mix. For pancakes and waffles, add about 1–1¼ cups water to 1 cup dry mix so the batter is pourable. You can add spices, herbs, dried cheese (like Parmesan), dried fruits, and nuts to create your own recipe variations. With the addition of seasoning, the mix is also good for coating fish and chicken before frying.

This recipe can be doubled and tripled for bulk baking.

I enjoy giving people gifts with a Rocky Mountain theme. In the past, I've made homemade pancake syrup using whatever fresh berry happens to be growing in abundance at that time of year. A jar of brightly colored syrup and a bag of this baking mix make a great Rocky Mountain gift for friends. I've also added dried huckleberries and cherries to the mix when giving it as a gift, or when carrying it in my backpack for a lightweight meal during a hiking trip. If you use stream water, don't forget to filter, boil, or treat it; cooking the pancakes or biscuits from the mix may not require enough heat to kill possible bacteria found in the water.

CARROT-BANANA BRAN MUFFINS

1 cup miller's bran

½ cup unbleached white flour

½ cup gluten (high protein) flour

1 teaspoon baking soda

2 teaspoons baking powder

¾ teaspoon salt

½ teaspoon ground cinnamon

½ teaspoon ground ginger

1 banana, mashed

6 tablespoons apple juice concentrate

3 tablespoons honey

1 tablespoon molasses

1 cup grated carrot

1 cup lowfat buttermilk

1 teaspoon vanilla

3 tablespoons safflower oil

1 egg

Preheat the oven to 400°. Grease a muffin pan that has 12 3-inch muffin cups.

Combine the dry ingredients in one bowl and the wet ingredients, including the banana and carrot, in another bowl, mixing each well. Fold the wet ingredients into the dry ingredients and stir until the mixture is just moistened.

Drop spoonfuls into muffin cups and bake for about 20 minutes, until firm to the touch.

Makes 12 muffins.

As you can see by the list of ingredients, I try to put as much healthy goodness in my muffins as possible. While a simple berry muffin may taste perfectly delicious, I always think of all the vitamin- and protein-packed ingredients I could have added to a batch of white-flour huckleberry muffins. It's an odd obsession, and I reserve it for muffins alone. I play around with muffin recipes, substituting a variety of whole grain flours for the more typical white flour. Dried fruits and nuts can also be added to batter without changing its baking properties. Many recipes contain fat, which I try to eliminate by using moist substitutes like apple sauce, nonfat yogurt, nonfat buttermilk, or mashed bananas to hold the dry ingredients together. You can cut out white sugar and make a more vitamin-rich muffin by using apple juice concentrate, honey, date powder, or molasses.

BEER BREAD WITH PARMESAN AND BASIL

2 cups unbleached white flour

3 teaspoons baking powder

³/₄ teaspoon salt

¹/₂ teaspoon dried basil leaves or
    1 teaspoon minced fresh basil

¹/₄ teaspoon coarsely ground black pepper

¹/₂ cup grated fresh Parmesan cheese

¹/₄ cup olive oil

³/₄ cup flat beer or ale

1 egg, lightly beaten

¹/₄ cup buttermilk

Preheat the oven to 400°. Grease a loaf pan.

In a large mixing bowl, combine the flour, baking powder, salt, basil, pepper, and Parmesan, stirring well.

Whisk the remaining ingredients together in a separate bowl. Fold the 2 mixtures together until moistened.

Pour the batter into the greased loaf pan and bake for about 45 minutes or until golden and firm to the touch. Cool in the pan for 15 minutes then remove. This bread is best served warm.

Makes 1 loaf.

Now that micro-breweries are plentiful in Rocky Mountain states like Montana, Colorado, and New Mexico, as well as in British Columbia, Canada, recipes using beer are showing up on restaurant menus and in cooking magazines with increased regularity. It takes some playing around, but you can substitute beer for a portion of the liquid ingredients in any stew or sauce recipe. To begin, try a ¹/₂ cup of beer in a creamed soup in place of a portion of the milk. Or, use beer instead of part of the beef broth or tomato sauce in a recipe for Swiss Steak.

SWEET POTATO BISCUITS

1 1/2 cups unbleached white flour

1/2 cup whole wheat flour

1/2 teaspoon allspice

1 tablespoon baking powder

1/2 teaspoon baking soda

3/4 teaspoon salt

1/4 cup chilled butter, cut into small pieces

3/4 cup cooked, mashed sweet potato

1/2 cup buttermilk

Preheat the oven to 425°.

Combine the flours, allspice, baking powder, baking soda, and salt in a mixing bowl. Cut the butter into the dry ingredients with a pastry knife or combine in a food processor until the mix has the consistency of cornmeal. Stir in the mashed sweet potato and buttermilk until a soft dough is formed.

Turn the dough onto a floured surface and gently knead just until it comes together in cohesive ball. Roll the dough to 1/2-inch thickness and cut out biscuits with a floured biscuit cutter or the rim of a drinking glass.

Place the biscuits close together on an ungreased baking sheet. Bake for 10–12 minutes or until the biscuits are golden. Serve immediately.

Makes 8–10 biscuits.

A recipe for sweet potato biscuits may seem an impossible stretch for a Rocky Mountain cookbook. Still, it's here, thanks to memorable characters like Montana's legendary Mary Fields, a former slave from the South who moved west and eventually opened a restaurant in Cascade, Montana. Other southerners also made their way to the Rockies in the 1800s and popularized southern staples like sweet potatoes and biscuits.

I like to use this recipe for holiday meals. The mashed sweet potatoes in the dough make these biscuits especially tender.

SOURDOUGH STARTER

1 package active dry yeast
2¹/₄ cups very warm water (120°)
2 cups unbleached white flour
2 tablespoons honey

In a mixing bowl, dissolve the yeast in ¹/₃ cup of the warm water. Add the remaining water, the flour, and the honey, whisking until smooth.

Cover the bowl with cotton cloth and let stand at room temperature for 6–8 days, stirring 2 times daily until the batter smells very sour.

Once it's fermented, pour the batter into a quart jar. Cover with a cotton cloth held in place by a rubber band. Refrigerate. Do not seal the jar with a tight-fitting lid.

If the starter isn't used within 10 days, add another teaspoon of honey. Repeat this step every 10 days until starter is used. This recipe makes about 2 cups of starter.

To use the starter, bring the required amount to room temperature. For each cup of starter you use, stir ³/₄ cup unbleached flour, ³/₄ cup water, and 1 teaspoon honey into the rest of the batter in the quart jar. Cover and let stand at room temperature until it bubbles— at least 24–48 hours. Refrigerate and proceed as before.

SOURDOUGH BASQUE SHEEPHERDER'S BREAD

2 tablespoons very warm water (110°)

1 package active dry yeast

1 cup milk

¼ cup vegetable oil

1½ cups sourdough starter
(see recipe on page 154)

2 tablespoons sugar

5 cups unbleached white flour

½ teaspoon salt

Combine the warm water and yeast, stirring to dissolve. Set aside.

Combine the milk and oil in a small saucepan and heat until very warm, about 115°.

With a wooden spoon or a whisk, beat together the dissolved yeast, milk mixture, sourdough starter, sugar, 2 cups of the flour, and the salt until smooth. Add enough of the remaining flour to make a stiff dough.

Turn the dough onto a floured surface and knead for 5–10 minutes, until smooth and elastic. Place the dough in a greased bowl, cover loosely, and let rise in a warm place for 1 hour or until doubled.

Preheat the oven to 350°. Thoroughly grease a Dutch oven and its lid (or any oven-proof lidded pan) with vegetable oil.

Punch down the dough and form it into a ball. Put it in the greased Dutch oven in a warm place, covered, and let rise again for about 30 minutes.

Bake the bread with the lid on the pot for 15 minutes. Remove the lid and bake for another 30 minutes. Cool for 5 minutes in the pan, then remove.

Makes 1 loaf.

I don't pretend to be an expert at this old method of using yeast to make your baked goods rise as well as to add a tangy sour flavor. I'm too absent-minded to keep that jar of sourdough starter in the back of my fridge going for longer than two weeks. I admire people who still have their grandmother's original starter going after fifty years, and I envy the superb flavor of their bread.

BLUE CORN MUFFINS WITH CHILIES

1 1/2 cups blue cornmeal

2 cups unbleached white flour

1/4 cup sugar

4 teaspoons baking powder

3/4 teaspoon salt

1/2 teaspoon red pepper flakes

2 eggs, lightly beaten

1 1/2 cups milk

1/4 cup oil

1 7-ounce can diced green chilies

1/2 cup finely shredded cheddar cheese

Preheat the oven to 400°. Grease a muffin pan containing 18–24 3-inch muffin cups.

Combine the dry ingredients in one bowl and the wet ingredients in another, stirring each well. Mix the 2 sets of ingredients together, stirring just until moistened.

Using a spoon, fill each muffin cup 2/3 full of batter. Bake for 15–20 minutes, until golden. Remove the muffins from the pan and serve warm.

Makes 18–24 muffins.

I had one of the most satisfying meals I've ever tasted after a late October trip to Santa Fe. I came home with a giant bag of fresh New Mexican green chilies and stood in the snow by my backyard barbecue, roasting peppers for a stew. To accent the stew, I made blue corn muffins. Try the following menu for a taste of the Southwest.

Suggested Menu:

- **Green Salad with Balsamic Vinaigrette (page 49)**
- **Green Chili Stew (page 27)**
- **Blue Corn Muffins with Chilies**
- **Dried Apple Whole Wheat Charlotte (page 125)**

WHOLE WHEAT-RED PEPPER TORTILLAS

1½ cups whole wheat flour

½ cup unbleached white flour

½ teaspoon cayenne pepper

1 teaspoon baking powder

¾ teaspoon salt

3 tablespoons lard or vegetable shortening

½ cup plus 2 tablespoons warm water

Combine the flours, cayenne, baking powder, and salt in a mixing bowl, stirring well. Cut in the lard or shortening with a pastry knife, or use a food processor. Gradually add ½ cup of the water until the dough can be formed into a ball. If you need to increase the amount of water, add 1 more tablespoon at a time.

Knead the dough 10–15 times, then let it rest for 10 minutes.

Divide the dough into 12 equal pieces and shape each piece into a round ball. Using a rolling pin, roll each ball on a lightly floured surface until it is very thin and about 8 inches in diameter. Stack the tortillas between waxed paper to prevent drying.

Preheat an ungreased griddle or skillet to medium-high.

One at a time, place the tortillas on the griddle. Cook the first side for about 30 seconds, until the tortilla begins to puff. Flip it and cook the other side for 30 seconds. Serve the tortillas immediately or wrap them in an airtight bag with waxed paper between them.

Makes 12 tortillas.

Making your own flour tortillas really isn't much trouble, and the hot-off-the-griddle reward is well worth the effort. I realized that it was easy to play around with tortilla recipes when I saw a woman at the Great Falls, Montana, farmers' market selling five different kinds of tortillas, including savory chocolate tortillas.

I learned to make this Southwest staple at the Santa Fe Cooking School. Authentic tortillas contain a great deal of real lard. This recipe calls for much less, and I usually use vegetable shortening.

MU SHU WRAPPERS

2½ cups unbleached white flour
½ teaspoon salt
1 cup boiling water
3 tablespoons sesame oil

Combine the flour and salt in a medium-sized mixing bowl. Pour in a cup of boiling water and stir until the mixture holds together. Turn the dough onto a floured surface and knead until smooth, about 10 minutes. Cover and let rest for 20 minutes.

With your hands, roll the dough into a foot-long log. Cut the log into 12 equal pieces. Then cut each piece in half. Roll the halves into balls and flatten each ball. Using a rolling pin, roll out the balls into 3-inch rounds.

Put an ungreased frying pan or griddle on medium heat. Brush sesame oil on one side of each wrapper and cook for about 15 seconds, until it begins to blister but not to brown. Do not cook the other side. Serve warm by folding in half and then in half again. Or cool the wrappers, place them in an airtight bag, and refrigerate them for up to 4 days. To reheat, fold the wrappers into a wet towel and warm them in a 250° oven, being careful not to let them become dry; or, steam them.

Makes 12 wrappers.

This Mu Shu pancake, or wrapper, is traditionally used to wrap up Chinese Mu Shu Pork filling. Cooks living in large cities can often find these wrappers in the freezer section of regular markets or in Asian food markets, but many of us must make our own. This recipe is just the beginning of a tasty meal—try it with Mu Shu Pork (page 82).

WALNUT, GARLIC, AND SUN-DRIED TOMATO FOCCACIA

1 envelope active dry yeast
2 cups unbleached white flour
1/3 cup whole wheat flour
2 teaspoons sugar
1/2 teaspoon salt
1 cup very warm water (115°)
1 tablespoon extra virgin olive oil
1 clove fresh garlic, crushed

6 tablespoons coarsely diced, olive oil-packed sundried tomatoes
1 teaspoon chopped fresh rosemary leaves
1/4 teaspoon fresh-ground black pepper
1/4 cup walnuts

In a large mixing bowl, combine the yeast, 1/2 cup of the white flour, all the whole wheat flour, the sugar, and the salt. Add the water and beat the mixture with a whisk or spoon for about 5 minutes, until it is smooth and elastic. Add the olive oil, garlic, tomatoes, rosemary, pepper, and walnuts and mix well.

Using a large spoon and then your hands, work in as much of the additional white flour as needed to make a stiff dough. Turn the dough onto a floured surface and knead it until smooth, using additional flour if necessary. Place the mound of dough in a greased bowl, cover it loosely with a moist cloth, and let it rise in warm place for 30 minutes.

Preheat the oven to 400°. Dust a round baking sheet with cornmeal.

Punch down the dough and let it rest for 10 minutes. Then oil your fingers and press the dough into a 10-inch round on the baking sheet. Cover it again and let rise for 20 minutes in a warm place.

Press dimples all over the surface of the dough with your fingertips. Using a spray bottle, mist the surface of the bread with water. Also mist the inside of the oven. Bake the foccacia for 10 minutes. Mist the inside of the oven again and bake for an additional 25 minutes or until lightly browned. Cut into wedges and serve.

Makes 1.

When your tomato plants have gone blissfully berserk and you're resorting to making tomato pancakes just to use them up, drying is a wise option. Roma or any of the plum-style tomatoes work best because of their meatier texture.

To dry tomatoes: Slice them in half lengthwise and scoop out the seeds. Lay them cut-side down on paper towels or paper grocery bags to drain for about 30 minutes. Then arrange them close together, but not touching, on drying racks, which can be made from old frames and sheets or wire mesh. Place the racks in a safe place in the sun. The drying process can take a couple of days, or you can finish the tomatoes off in a 175–200° oven. Turn the tomatoes once during drying. Store in airtight bags or pack in jars with olive oil.

VEGETABLE-HERB DUMPLINGS

  2 cups all-purpose flour
  ³/₄ cup whole wheat flour
  2 tablespoons sugar
  3¹/₂ teaspoons baking powder
  1 teaspoon salt
  ¹/₂ teaspoon dried sage
  ¹/₂ teaspoon thyme
  ¹/₂ teaspoon parsley
  ¹/₂ cup melted butter
  2 eggs, lightly beaten
  1 cup buttermilk
  ¹/₂ cup frozen or fresh cut corn

  ¹/₄ cup diced red bell pepper
  ¹/₄ cup diced carrot
  ¹/₄ cup diced celery
  ¹/₄ cup diced red onion

In a large mixing bowl, mix the dry ingredients together well. Add the wet ingredients and vegetables and stir the mixture until combined.

Drop the dough by heaping tablespoons into any boiling soup, chili, or stew you are cooking on the stovetop. Cook uncovered for 10 minutes. Cover the pot and cook for another 10 minutes. Serve immediately.

Makes approximately 20 dumplings.

These dumplings were born of my habit of adding vegetables to just about any recipe I can—twice-baked potatoes, basic tuna and noodles, a plate of scrambled eggs, even pancakes. If I'm going to go to the trouble of making dumplings to add to a stew or chili, I figure I might as well add the extra flavor, texture, vitamins, and minerals that come from a few fresh veggies.

CHEDDAR BISCUITS WITH THYME AND SAGE

3 cups unbleached white flour

4 teaspoons baking powder

1 teaspoon salt

1/2 cup vegetable shortening

1 cup milk

1/2 teaspoon dried thyme or
   1 teaspoon fresh thyme

1/2 teaspoon dried sage or
   1 teaspoon fresh sage

2 cups grated extra-sharp cheddar cheese

1 egg yolk, beaten

Preheat the oven to 425°.

Mix the flour, baking powder, and salt in a large bowl. Cut in the shortening with a pastry knife until the mixture resembles coarse meal. Add the milk and herbs and mix until a moist dough forms. Using your hands, mix in the cheese.

Turn the dough onto a floured surface and knead gently 5 or 6 times to distribute the cheese. Using a rolling pin, roll out the dough to a 1/2-inch thickness. Cut out biscuits with a floured biscuit or cookie cutter and place them on an ungreased baking sheet. Brush the tops with beaten egg yolk.

Bake for 15 minutes or until golden. Serve warm.

Makes 12–14 biscuits.

Before an early August snow (yes, August; I've got pictures) obliterated my thriving Montana garden one year, I'd nearly harvested the biggest crop of fresh herbs I'd ever been fortunate enough to grow. I am not known for anything resembling a green thumb, although I keep trying to shake this reputation. But that year I was practically cocky about my vegetable garden, especially my herbs. As the chef at the Paris Gibson Square Museum of Art Conservatory in Great Falls, Montana, I had dreamed up several fresh-herb-themed menus for the summer. After searching out herbs that had survived the early snow, I prepared a duck salad with fresh lemon thyme and rosemary-crusted foccacia to go with these biscuits.

That summer taught me to harvest my herbs throughout the season. They will actually produce more, and you get to enjoy them regardless of when the first snow falls.

DRIED CRANBERRY–OAT SODA BREAD

3½ cups unbleached flour
½ cup sugar
1 teaspoon baking soda
1 tablespoon baking powder
½ teaspoon salt
¼ teaspoon cream of tartar
⅓ cup butter, melted
1 cup dried cranberries
½ cup rolled oats
2 eggs
1¾ cups buttermilk

Preheat the oven to 350°. Grease a 9-inch round pan or casserole.

Combine the flour, sugar, baking soda, powder, salt, and cream of tartar in a large mixing bowl. Add the butter and stir until the mixture becomes crumbly. Mix in the dried cranberries and oats.

In a separate bowl, beat the eggs into the buttermilk. Pour the wet ingredients into the dry ingredients and mix until well combined.

Form the dough into a round loaf and place in the greased pan. Bake for 70 minutes, until golden and firm. Cool on a wire rack.

Makes 1 loaf.

A lot of Irish miners, railroad workers, farmers, and loggers (not to mention my paternal grandparents and great-grandparents) survived on staples like soda bread and potatoes in the early years of the West. Even though I add a few ingredients they probably didn't have, the basic recipe is the same. Because of my very Irish heritage, creating recipes like this one is a nostalgic act.

SWEDISH RYE LIMPA WITH ANISEED AND CURRANTS

5 cups unbleached white flour

2¹/₂ cups rye flour

1 teaspoon salt

2 envelopes active dry yeast

1 teaspoon aniseed

2 tablespoons grated orange peel

2 tablespoons molasses

2³/₄ cups hot water (120°)

2 tablespoons vegetable oil

¹/₂ cup dried currants

In a large bowl, combine 4 cups of the white flour, the rye flour, and the salt, yeast, aniseed, and orange peel.

Blend the molasses into the hot water and stir in the oil. Pour these into the dry ingredients and mix well. Fold the currants into the mixture and add enough of the leftover cup of flour to form a soft dough.

Turn the dough onto a floured surface and knead for 10 minutes, until smooth. Place the dough in a greased bowl and cover loosely with plastic wrap. Let rise in a warm place for about 1 hour, until doubled in bulk. Punch down the dough and split into 2 balls. Place the balls on a greased baking sheet with space between them. Cover and let rise in a warm place for another hour.

Preheat the oven to 400°.

Slash the tops of the loaves. Bake for 35 minutes or until the loaves sound hollow when tapped on the bottom. Cool on a rack.

Makes 2 loaves.

This recipe inspires me to attempt to further explain the concept of Rocky Mountain gourmet. I will use the Swede-Finn Hall in Telluride, Colorado, to illustrate my point. This restaurant's menu offers such dishes as Athenian Chicken Pasta, Jamaican Jerk Chicken, Blackened Salmon, and Pan-Seared Elk with Wild Mushroom Sauce. Even the one Swedish dish on the menu has a less-than-traditional twist: the Linguini Swede-Finn is served with homemade meatballs along with more unusual (or Rocky Mountain) flavors such as red peppers, fennel, and garlic. Old standards—wonderful ethnic foods—are "dressed up" with Rocky Mountain flavors and ingredients. *Voila,* Rocky Mountain gourmet.

HUCKLEBERRY SWIRL BREAD

2 cups milk

¼ cup butter

⅔ cup sugar

1 teaspoon salt

2 packages active dry yeast

½ teaspoon cinnamon

3 cups unbleached white flour

3 cups whole wheat flour

2 eggs

½ cup mashed frozen, fresh, or canned huckleberries

1 egg, beaten with 1 tablespoon of water

Heat the milk, butter, sugar, and salt until very warm (120-130°).

In 2 separate bowls, 1 for white flour, 1 for whole wheat flour, combine 1 package of yeast, ¼ teaspoon cinnamon, and 1½ cups white or wheat flour (respectively). Add half the hot milk mixture and 1 egg to each bowl and beat well with a wooden spoon until the batters are smooth.

Turn both mounds of dough onto a floured board and work in as much of the remaining 1½ cups of flour (keep the white and wheat separate) as is necessary to make the doughs soft and smooth. Place each kind of dough in a greased bowl, cover, and let rise in a warm place for about 1 hour, until each has doubled. Punch down the doughs and let them rest for 10 minutes, covered.

Preheat the oven to 375°. Grease a baking sheet.

Shape each piece of dough into a rectangle about ½ inch thick. Cut each rectangle in half widthwise. Press mashed huckleberries into both pieces of white dough; cover each with a rectangle of wheat dough. Press the top and bottom pieces together and seal the edges. Roll up each rectangle lengthwise, pressing as you go, to form long loaves. Place the loaves seam side down on the greased baking sheet. Cover and let rise for about 30 minutes.

Brush the loaves with egg and bake for about 30 minutes or until golden and firm.

Makes 2 French-style swirl loaves.

When picking berries, take some additional time to make sure you don't waste your efforts because you haven't stored the berries properly. Pour freshly picked berries into heavy gallon-sized resealable plastic bags as you go. Lay the filled bags flat and don't stack them very high, so there isn't a lot of weight on the bottom berries.

Some people like to pour water into their sacks of berries before freezing them. I don't recommend this method. Freezing the berries dry and whole not only preserves their shape, but allows you to pour out as many berries as you need without thawing the entire bunch. Just press the excess air out of the bags before sealing and freezing them.

SAGE POPOVERS

1½ cups unbleached white flour

¼ teaspoon salt

1½ cups milk

4 eggs

4 tablespoons melted butter

¼ teaspoon finely ground black pepper

1½ teaspoons ground sage

non-stick cooking spray

Preheat the oven to 375°. Spray popover pans or ²/₃-cup custard cups with non-stick cooking spray.

Combine all the popover ingredients in a blender and blend for 30 seconds to a minute.

Heat the sprayed pan or cups in the oven for a couple of minutes until hot. Fill half full with batter. Bake for 40–45 minutes or until golden brown and crisp. Serve with stews or roast meats, especially wild game.

Makes 8 popovers.

For a hearty, mostly make-ahead menu (leave time for the last-minute preparation of the Sage Popover recipe on this page), the following selections will promise a variety of flavors and easy reheating after a day at the office or in the field. This is very much a comfort-food menu, so when you've got company coming for dinner on a chilly autumn night, serve it family-style for optimum coziness.

Suggested Menu:

- Zuni Posole Stew with Pork (page 20)
- Root Vegetables Au Gratin with Nutmeg (page 55)
- Basque Green Beans in Tomato Broth (page 58)
- Sage Popovers
- Huckleberry Bread Pudding (page 129)

POLENTA-PUMPKIN MADELEINES
WITH THYME

1 tablespoon polenta or yellow cornmeal

¼ cup finely minced onion

¼ cup butter or margarine

1 cup unbleached white flour

1 cup polenta or yellow cornmeal

1 tablespoon baking powder

½ teaspoon dried thyme or
   1 teaspoon fresh thyme

½ teaspoon salt

1 egg

1 cup milk

1 cup mashed pumpkin

non-stick cooking spray

Preheat the oven to 375°. Spray madeleine pans with non-stick cooking spray. Sprinkle the entire pan with the tablespoon of polenta, then shake out the excess.

Sauté the onion in the butter for about 3 minutes over medium heat in a frying pan.

In a mixing bowl, combine the flour, polenta, baking powder, thyme, and salt.

In a separate bowl, whisk the egg into the milk. Stir the onion-butter mixture and the mashed pumpkin into the milk-egg mixture, then add to the flour mixture, stirring until moistened.

Spoon about 2 tablespoons or less batter into each pan, filling them to the rims. Bake for about 12 minutes or until golden and firm to the touch. Let cool in the pans for 3 minutes then invert the pans to remove the madeleines, using the edge of a spatula if necessary.

Makes 2–3 dozen madeleines.

Most of the madeleines we see in bakeries or served at high tea in old hotels are sweet rather than savory. But the attractive shape of what amounts to a tiny muffin baked in a special shell-shaped pan makes madeleines appealing to serve warm or at room temperature as a savory accompaniment to salads and soups.

Just a hint—I've even used prepared muffin mixes, with a few extra ingredients thrown in, of course, for a quick extra when friends are coming for a bowl of chili. With prepared muffin mixes, it takes barely five minutes to put the ingredients together and just a bit more time to bake the madeleines.

Most cooking supply stores have French-inspired madeleine pans as do a number of baking catalogs.

SAVORY CHOCOLATE AND RED CHILI BREADSTICKS

1³/4 cups unbleached flour

¹/4 cup plus 3 tablespoons cocoa powder

1 envelope dry yeast

2 teaspoons sugar

¹/2 teaspoon salt

³/4 teaspoon red pepper flakes

1 cup hot water (120°–130°)

1 tablespoon canola oil

extra flour and cocoa powder combined
    for kneading

cornmeal for coating baking sheet

Combine the flour, cocoa, yeast, sugar, salt, and red pepper flakes in a mixing bowl. Pour the hot water and oil into the flour mixture, stirring well to form a smooth dough.

Turn the dough onto a cocoa-floured surface. Knead in additional cocoa flour to form a soft dough. Knead for about 5–10 minutes until smooth and elastic. Place the dough in an oiled bowl, cover loosely with plastic wrap, and let rise in a warm place for about 45 minutes, until doubled.

Preheat the oven to 350°. Grease a baking sheet and dust it with cornmeal.

Punch down the dough and let it rest for 5 minutes. Divide it with a knife into 8 equal pieces. Use your hands to roll each piece into a rope. Twist each rope from both ends (in opposite directions) and place on the baking sheet. Cover and let rise again in a warm place for 15 minutes. Bake for about 15 minutes, until crisp and firm to the touch.

Makes 10 breadsticks.

Ever since I tried the ancient Mexican mole sauce, which combines chocolate, nuts, and hot chili peppers, I've been addicted to its mix of flavors. I even tried a fudge sauce that had habañero chilies hiding in it poured over vanilla bean ice cream. But I'm not really one of those people who can handle hot chilies without a little help—so I sought out this marriage of chocolate and chilies. When the barbed spike of the chilies hits the tongue, the chocolate arrives just in time to soothe.

A fun addition to a meal centered around stew or chili is a basket full of three or four kinds of homemade breadsticks—try whole wheat-carrot, spinach-garlic, and these chocolate and red chili breadsticks with their deep, rich color to jazz up your meal. Test other varieties by replacing the cocoa powder and seasonings in this recipe with equal amounts of your own creative ingredients.

BRUNCH

Smoked Salmon Frittata

Calabria-Style Eggs in a Nest

Gingerbread Pancakes with Huckleberry Sauce

Polenta Triangles with Poached Eggs, Peppers, and Hollandaise

Asparagus and Almond Quiche

Prime Rib Hash

Country Potato Cakes with Vegetable Coulis

Corn-Browned Trout Stuffed with Green Chilies and Eggs

Five-Grain Flap Jacks with Applesauce

Breakfast Lasagne with Spinach, Almonds, and Eggs

Apple and Cheddar Strudel

Banana-Bran Pancakes with Fresh Berries

Lowfat Fruity Granola

Black Bean and Potato Breakfast Burritos

Blue Corn Biscuits with Sausage-Apple Gravy

Baked Oatmeal Custard with Dried Apricots and Almonds

Spiced Dutch Baby with Dried-Apple Sauce

Chocolate-Raspberry French Toast

Chokecherry Syrup

SMOKED SALMON FRITTATA

4 cups cubed French bread—
   sliced into 1-inch cubes

1 cup flaked smoked salmon or another
   variety of smoked fish

6 eggs, lightly whisked

5 cups milk (1% or 2% milkfat)

1/2 cup grated fresh Parmesan cheese

1 clove garlic, crushed

1 teaspoon Italian seasoning

1/2 teaspoon salt

1/2 teaspoon freshly ground black pepper

1/2 cup diced red bell pepper

1/2 cup diced green onion

1/2 cup diced carrot

1/2 cup diced zucchini

non-stick cooking spray

Measure all the ingredients except the vegetables into a mixing bowl. Fold with a spatula until well combined. Set aside so the bread cubes can absorb the liquid.

Preheat the oven to 350°.

Toss the vegetables in a sauté pan with a tablespoon of water. Cook over medium heat for 2–3 minutes. Remove from heat and let cool.

Lightly coat a 9 x 13-inch baking pan with non-stick spray.

Fold the cooled vegetables into the egg mixture and pour the batter into the baking pan. Bake for 35–40 minutes, until the egg mixture is set and no longer runny. Serve immediately.

Serves 6.

Frittatas are an Italian version of quiche and the popular breakfast casseroles we usually see filled with ham or sausage. I like this recipe because it's lighter than either quiche or egg casserole, yet retains the coziness of a warm and eggy brunch entrée. The smoky flavor of the salmon mirrors the taste of traditional breakfast meats like ham, bacon, and sausage, but without all the grease.

You'll often see frittata sliced into wedges in the refrigerator cases of Italian delis. Italians may consider this more of a lunch or dinner entrée. Try serving it with salad and a crusty bread as a light meal later in the day. For brunch, serve it with a bowl of fresh fruit and orange juice-champagne mimosas.

CALABRIA-STYLE EGGS IN A NEST

Sauce:

1 tablespoon extra virgin olive oil

2 tablespoons finely minced onion

1 cup diced roma tomatoes

1 teaspoon sugar

2 tablespoons fresh basil

salt and pepper to taste

Egg Nests:

6 tablespoons butter

1 clove garlic, crushed

8 1/2-inch-thick slices of heavy Italian or French bread with a 2-inch-diameter hole cut from the middle of each slice

8 large eggs

1/2 cup grated Parmesan cheese

salt and pepper to taste

1/4 cup ricotta cheese for garnish

For the sauce: Heat the olive oil in a small saucepan over medium heat. Sauté the onions until wilted. Add the tomatoes, sugar, and basil and cook, stirring, for about 5 more minutes. Season with salt and pepper. Cover and keep warm while preparing the egg nests.

For the egg nests: Prepare the bread, ready the ingredients, and preheat a griddle to medium-high heat. Melt half the butter on the griddle. Stir half the crushed garlic into the butter for about 1 minute, spreading the mixture around the surface of the griddle.

Lay 4 slices of bread in the butter. Break 1 egg into the center of each piece of bread and cook for about 3 minutes. Sprinkle with Parmesan cheese, salt, and pepper and flip over carefully. Cook for another minute.

Repeat with the other half of the ingredients and the additional 4 pieces of bread.

Arrange 2 nests on each plate. Ladle a spoonful of the warm tomato sauce over them. Serve with a dollop of ricotta cheese on top.

Serves 4.

This is a dressed-up version of a common peasant breakfast that Italian children enjoyed for centuries. It was cheap, used up day-old bread, and included eggs as a hearty source of protein. Calabria, Italy, is where my daughter Tessa's Great-Grandma Nicki is from, and Nicki is the first person I heard describe this traditional Italian dish.

You can use half as much dry basil in the sauce with delicious results, but I consider this dish a prime showcase for fresh summer basil, because there aren't too many other flavors. I press out the center of the slices of bread with a juice glass to make the holes for the eggs.

GINGERBREAD PANCAKES WITH HUCKLEBERRY SAUCE

Huckleberry Sauce:

$1/4$ cup granulated sugar

1 tablespoon cornstarch

1 teaspoon lemon juice

$3/4$ cup apple juice

1 cup huckleberry jam

Gingerbread Pancakes:

$1\frac{1}{2}$ cups unbleached white flour

$3/4$ cup whole wheat flour

1 teaspoon salt

1 teaspoon baking soda

4 teaspoons baking powder

1 teaspoon ground ginger

$1/2$ teaspoon ground cloves

1 teaspoon ground cinnamon

$1/3$ cup molasses

$2\frac{1}{4}$ cups milk

2 eggs, slightly beaten

5 tablespoons butter, melted

Combine all the ingredients for the sauce in a saucepan. Cook over medium heat, whisking continuously, until the sauce bubbles. Reduce the heat to low and stir until smooth and thickened. Remove from heat and cover to keep warm.

To make the pancakes, combine the flours, salt, baking soda, baking powder, and spices in a mixing bowl. In separate bowl, whisk together the molasses, milk, eggs, and butter. Pour this mixture into the dry ingredients and stir only until moistened.

Cook the pancakes on a hot griddle, using about $1/4$ cup of batter for each pancake. Top with warm huckleberry sauce.

Serves 6–8.

If you've got a big group coming for brunch, the following menu is hefty enough to fill many appetites. Make the fruit soup ahead and chill it in a pitcher in the refrigerator, ready to be poured into clear glass bowls as people arrive. The hash can be all done and warming in the oven while you pour the batter onto the griddle for fresh gingerbread pancakes. The asparagus can be finished at the last minute on the stovetop.

Suggested Menu:

- Scandinavian Berry Fruit Soup with Cinnamon (page 30)
- Asparagus with Toasted Hazelnuts and Garlic (page 54)
- Gingerbread Pancakes with Huckleberry Sauce
- Prime Rib Hash (page 175)

POLENTA TRIANGLES WITH POACHED EGGS, PEPPERS, AND HOLLANDAISE

Polenta Triangles:

3 1/2 cups water

1/2 teaspoon salt

1 cup polenta or coarsely ground cornmeal

1/4 cup grated Parmesan cheese

1 tablespoon extra virgin olive oil

Pepper Topping:

1 tablespoon olive oil

1 red bell pepper, julienned

1/4 cup diced green scallions

1 clove garlic, crushed

Hollandaise Sauce:

3 egg yolks at room temperature

1 tablespoon water

pinch of salt

2/3 cup butter, melted

pinch of cayenne pepper

1 1/2 teaspoons fresh lemon juice (or to taste)

salt and pepper to taste

8 eggs

Grease a 9 x 13-inch baking pan. In a medium saucepan, bring the water and salt to a boil. Gradually stir in the polenta. Reduce the heat and simmer on low for 15 minutes, stirring constantly. Stir in the Parmesan cheese and 1 tablespoon of the olive oil. Pour the polenta into the greased pan to about a 3/4-inch thickness. Let stand for about 20 minutes to thicken (or refrigerate if you won't be using it that day). Cut it into squares and then into triangles. Warm the polenta in the oven while preparing the toppings and the eggs.

Make the pepper topping next. Heat the olive oil in a small frying pan. Sauté the peppers, scallions, and garlic for 3 minutes and set aside.

For the sauce, blend the 3 egg yolks with the water and salt for 2 minutes in a blender or food processor. Gradually pour the melted butter into the egg yolks, a small amount at a time, still mixing. Finally, blend in the cayenne and lemon juice. Taste to see if more salt, cayenne, or lemon juice is needed. Set aside for a short time only while poaching the eggs.

To poach the eggs, heat 2 inches of water in a skillet to a slow simmer. Squeeze a few drops of lemon juice into the water. Crack the eggs one by one, sliding each egg gently into the simmering water. Poach, uncovered, for 3 minutes. Check to see that the white is firm. Remove the eggs carefully with slotted spoon and drain over a paper towel. Lay each egg on top of a warm polenta triangle.

Place two polenta-egg stacks on each plate. Spoon hollandaise sauce on top of the eggs and scatter some of the pepper mixture on top, dividing the peppers between the 4 plates.

Serves 4.

To speed up the preparation of this meal, prepare the polenta a day ahead, slice it, and have it warming in the oven while you put together the rest of the dish.

ASPARAGUS AND ALMOND QUICHE

½ pound fresh, thin asparagus, trimmed and
   cut into 1-inch pieces

1 tablespoon butter

¼ cup diced scallions

½ cup slivered almonds

½ teaspoon thyme

½ teaspoon marjoram

¼ teaspoon freshly grated nutmeg

4 large eggs

1½ cups half-and-half

½ pound Swiss cheese, grated

¼ teaspoon salt

⅛ teaspoon freshly ground black pepper

1 9-inch unbaked pie shell

Preheat the oven to 375°.

Melt the butter in a small skillet over medium heat. Sauté the asparagus pieces for 3 minutes. Remove them from the heat and pour them into a mixing bowl.

Add all the remaining ingredients and whisk until well blended. Pour the batter into the uncooked pie shell and bake for 35–40 minutes, or until a knife inserted in the center comes out clean. Let sit for 15 minutes before serving.

Makes 1 quiche.

Although I have not included a recipe for pie crust here, I recommend trying one of the numerous, very simple pie crust recipes found in most general, standard cookbooks. You can use white, wheat, or mixed-grain flour to make the crust for this quiche.

PRIME RIB HASH

4 tablespoons butter

1 clove garlic, crushed

1 large red onion, diced

¼ cup diced celery

½ cup diced red bell pepper

3 cups leftover prime rib or steak, precooked and cubed

2 pounds red-skinned potatoes, cubed, boiled for 10 minutes, and drained

⅛ cup minced fresh parsley

½ teaspoon thyme

¼ teaspoon sage

salt and pepper to taste

4–6 eggs

Melt the butter in a large non-stick frying pan over medium-high heat. Add the garlic, onion, celery, and red pepper. Sauté until the vegetables soften, about 8 minutes. Add the prime rib, potatoes, parsley, thyme, and sage and stir well to combine. Continue cooking, stirring frequently, for about 5–10 minutes, depending on the level of browning desired. Add the salt and pepper to taste.

Break 4–6 eggs on top of the hash. Cover the pan and let the eggs cook for 3–5 minutes.

Serves 4–6.

This recipe is similar to one found on old dining stop menus. The first transcontinental travelers to venture into Ogden didn't have the luxury of dining cars. For several years, rail travelers ate at dining stations during quick thirty-minute stops. Recipes like this Prime Rib Hash were better suited to the "fast food" requirements of 1880s rail travelers.

COUNTRY POTATO CAKES WITH VEGETABLE COULIS

Coulis:

1 tablespoon extra virgin olive oil

¼ cup finely minced red onion

1 clove garlic, crushed

½ cup finely minced red bell pepper

¼ cup frozen corn

½ cup finely diced zucchini

1 cup diced fresh tomatoes

1 tablespoon sugar

¼ teaspoon sage

½ teaspoon crushed rosemary

salt and pepper to taste

⅛ teaspoon cayenne pepper

2 tablespoons ketchup

Potato Cakes:

5 large russet potatoes, baked for 30 minutes so still firm, peeled, and shredded

½ cup finely minced onion

1 clove garlic, crushed

1 cup fine dry bread crumbs

2 eggs

½ teaspoon thyme

salt and pepper to taste

4 tablespoons butter

To prepare the coulis, heat the olive oil in a medium-sized sauce pan over medium heat. Sauté the vegetables, stirring frequently, until they begin to wilt—about 5 minutes. Add the remaining sauce ingredients, stir, and cover the pot. Reduce heat to low and cook for 10 minutes. Set aside while preparing the potato cakes.

In a medium-sized mixing bowl, combine all the ingredients for the potato cakes except the butter. Form the cakes with your hands: for each cake, pat ½ cup of the potato mixture to a ¾-inch thickness.

Melt half of the butter in a large non-stick skillet. Brown half of the patties on both sides. Set them aside on a plate. Melt the other half of the butter and brown the rest of the patties. Spoon the vegetable coulis sauce over the potato cakes and serve.

Serves 4.

I always keep a large bag of potatoes in the cupboard under my kitchen sink. A potato is an incredible root: it's nourishing and can be prepared in a great many ways.

It's surprising how many heirloom photographs there are in state historical society archives that depict people peeling potatoes: children propped up on chairs next to a table full of potatoes; old men crouched next to chuck wagons peeling their daily ration of spuds; women gathered around in a circle dropping peeled potatoes into a giant pot for a church supper. Although we think of potatoes as a cheap food, residents of some mining camps in the late 1800s had to fork out as much as $20 for a sack of the simple brown roots.

CORN-BROWNED TROUT STUFFED WITH GREEN CHILIES AND EGGS

Chili Filling:
   1 tablespoon butter
$^1/_4$ cup finely diced onion
   1 clove garlic, crushed
$^1/_8$ cup minced cilantro leaves
$^1/_4$ teaspoon crushed red pepper flakes
   1 cup canned diced green chilies
$^1/_2$ cup grated Monterey jack cheese

Trout:
$^1/_2$ lime
   8 trout fillets, 5–8 ounces each
toothpicks

$^1/_4$ cup cornmeal
$^1/_4$ cup all-purpose flour
salt and pepper to taste

   3 tablespoons butter or non-stick cooking
      spray

Eggs:
   8 eggs
$^1/_4$ teaspoon cumin
$^1/_2$ teaspoon oregano
salt and pepper to taste

salsa for garnish

To prepare the filling, heat the butter in a small skillet over medium heat. Sauté the onion for 5 minutes. Add the garlic, cilantro, red pepper flakes, and green chilies. Stir to blend. Remove from the heat and mix in the grated cheese.

Squeeze the lime over the fish fillets. Lay 1 trout fillet on a plate and cover it with $^1/_4$ of the chili filling. Cover with a second trout fillet and secure the sides with toothpicks. Repeat with the rest of the fillets and filling. In a small bowl, combine the cornmeal, flour, salt, and pepper. Sprinkle half the mixture over the trout fillets and pat it against the flesh of the fish so that it adheres. Turn the fillets over carefully and sprinkle the other side with the cornmeal mixture.

Heat a large skillet over medium-high heat and coat it with the butter or cooking spray. Lay the fillets in the skillet . Brown the first side for about 5 minutes. You may need to reduce the heat if they brown too quickly. Carefully turn the fillets with a spatula and brown the other side. Cover the pan with a lid, turn the heat to low, and let the trout finish cooking—about 5 more minutes. Place the cooked fish in a warm oven until you are ready to serve them.

Mix the eggs with the cumin, oregano, salt, and pepper. Scramble them over medium-low heat.

Spoon the eggs over the trout on individual plates and garnish with salsa.

Serves 4.

Freshwater trout is a frequent breakfast ingredient on backcountry camping trips, but it is also delicious in more elegant settings. I like it because it is much lighter than more traditional breakfast meats like sausage and bacon.

FIVE-GRAIN FLAPJACKS WITH APPLESAUCE

³/₄ cup unbleached white flour

³/₄ cup whole wheat flour

¹/₄ cup cornmeal

¹/₂ cup old-fashioned rolled oats

¹/₄ cup finely ground pecans (grind in a food processor or blender)

2 tablespoons baking powder

¹/₂ teaspoon cinnamon

3 tablespoons brown sugar

¹/₂ teaspoon salt

2 eggs, lightly beaten

2¹/₂ cups milk

4 tablespoons vegetable oil

2 cups applesauce

pecan halves

Combine the dry ingredients in one bowl and the eggs, milk, and oil in a separate, smaller bowl, mixing each well. Pour the wet ingredients into the dry and stir just until moistened.

Grease a heated griddle. Use a ¹/₄-cup measure to pour the batter for each pancake onto the griddle. Cook until golden on both sides.

Serve topped with applesauce and a few pecan halves.

Serves 4.

Where did pancakes, sometimes called griddle cakes or flapjacks, come from? While many are ready to take the credit, the story most often goes like this:

Cooks in the early western lumber camps didn't usually have much in the way of cooking equipment: waffle irons, muffin pans, and ovens for baking biscuits weren't a part of their kitchen package. Someone figured out that if they thinned down a biscuit or muffin recipe, they could pour the batter right on a griddle placed on some rocks over dwindling coals. It was easy to make a lot of these little cakes. They were easy to serve with a little molasses or berry syrup, and they were filling. First called flannel cakes, for the flannel shirts worn by the lumberjacks in the camps, they also became known as flats, because of the flatcars that carried the fresh-cut lumber to market.

BREAKFAST LASAGNE WITH SPINACH, ALMONDS, AND EGGS

1/2 cup finely diced onion

2 tablespoons extra virgin olive oil

2 cloves garlic, crushed

2 tablespoons butter

2 tablespoons all-purpose flour

3 tablespoons sherry

3 cups half-and-half

1 teaspoon Italian seasoning

1/2 teaspoon salt

1/4 teaspoon freshly ground black pepper

4 cups firmly packed, finely chopped fresh spinach leaves

8 sheets of lasagne noodles, cooked and drained

2 cups ricotta cheese

1 cup freshly grated Parmesan cheese

8 eggs, scrambled in 1 tablespoon of butter until still runny in consistency

1/2 cup slivered almonds

non-stick cooking spray

Preheat the oven to 350°. Spray a 9 x 13-inch inch baking pan with non-stick cooking spray.

In a medium-sized saucepan, cook the onions in the olive oil for 3 minutes. Add the garlic and butter and cook another 2 minutes, stirring frequently. Stir the flour into the onion mixture until well dissolved. Whisk in the sherry, then the half-and-half, 1/2 cup at a time, stirring to prevent lumps. Cook until bubbly, smooth, and thickened. Add the Italian seasoning, salt, pepper, and spinach. Stir to combine and set aside.

To assemble the lasagne: Pour a few spoonfuls of spinach sauce into the bottom of the prepared pan. Lay 4 lasagne noodles on top, side by side, overlapping the edges. Pour a third of the remaining spinach sauce over the noodles. Spread all the ricotta over the sauce. Sprinkle half the Parmesan over the ricotta, then lay the other 4 lasagne noodles on top. Pour the second third of the spinach sauce over this layer. Spoon all the scrambled eggs over the sauce and top that layer with the almonds, then final third of the sauce. Sprinkle with the rest of the Parmesan cheese.

Bake until the top begins to turn golden, about 45 minutes. Serve immediately.

Serves 4–6.

This breakfast casserole is especially popular with my vegetarian friends. I enjoy its light quality, which contrasts with so many sausage- and bacon-laden morning casseroles. It's a terrific carry-along breakfast for a weekend of skiing or fishing at a mountain lodge with a group of friends. Underbake the lasagne by 15 minutes, wrap it well in foil, and freeze the whole works. When you're ready to share the meal, thaw and reheat at 350° for 30 minutes or until bubbling and heated through.

APPLE AND CHEDDAR STRUDEL

5 Granny Smith apples, peeled, cored, and sliced into thin wedges

8 tablespoons butter, melted

1 teaspoon cornstarch

2 tablespoons brown sugar

1 tablespoon lemon juice

1 teaspoon cinnamon

6 tablespoons maple syrup

2 8-ounce packages cream cheese

2 egg yolks

2 cups grated sharp cheddar cheese

16 sheets phyllo pastry dough

Preheat the oven to 375°. Grease a baking sheet.

In large skillet, toss the apple slices in 2 tablespoons of the butter for 3 minutes over medium heat. Add the cornstarch, brown sugar, lemon juice, and cinnamon. Toss and cook for another 3–5 minutes until well incorporated. Remove the apple mixture from the heat and set aside.

Using an electric mixer, beat the maple syrup into the cream cheese until fluffy. Add the egg yolks and beat until incorporated.

Fold the apple mixture and the sharp cheddar into the cream cheese mixture.

Lay 2 sheets of phyllo dough on top of a sheet of waxed paper. Brush with melted butter. Add another phyllo sheet, brush with butter; add 1 more sheet and brush with butter; and repeat 4 more times until 8 sheets have been used. Spread half the apple filling along one edge of the stack of buttered phyllo sheets, leaving a 1-inch border. Roll up the sheets like a jelly roll. Place the seam side down on the greased baking sheet. Brush the top of the roll with butter. Slice a couple of knife scores in the top of the strudel. Repeat all steps for a second roll.

Bake for about 20 minutes until golden. Cool and slice into rounds.

Serves 6–8.

Phyllo is a great option for people trying to cut down on fat. Replace fat-laden pie dough with 5–8 phyllo sheets, using a touch of non-stick cooking spray between the sheets. Mold the phyllo into a pie pan, trim the edges with scissors, and you've got a light and easy base for a quiche or apple pie.

BANANA-BRAN PANCAKES WITH FRESH BERRIES

1/4 cup vegetable oil

2 eggs, lightly beaten

2 cups milk

1 teaspoon vanilla

2 ripe bananas, mashed

3/4 cup millers bran

1 cup unbleached white flour

1/2 cup whole wheat flour

2 tablespoons sugar

1 1/2 teaspoons baking powder

1/2 teaspoon salt

2 cups fresh berries in season, single kind or a combination

non-stick cooking spray

Combine the wet ingredients in one bowl and the dry ingredients in another. Stir each well, taking care to break up the mashed banana. Pour the wet ingredients into the flour mixture. Stir just until moistened.

Grease a griddle with non-stick cooking spray and heat to medium-high temperature.

Pour the batter onto the griddle, 1/4 cup per cake. Cook the pancakes until golden, flip, and cook the other side. Serve with sliced fresh berries on top.

Serves 6–8.

Oddly enough, banana pancakes make me think of fishing. The first time I ever went fly fishing was also the first time I had banana pancakes. I fell in love with both. A friend made banana pancakes for me before we headed out for a rainy day of fly fishing on Montana's Madison and Gallatin rivers. I'm into anything banana: banana bread, banana chips, banana splits, dried bananas, banana shakes—you get the idea. So it was no surprise that I was thoroughly enthralled with bananas in flapjack form. As for the fishing that day, I didn't catch a single one. But I learned how to fish riffles, how to tie a fly on my line while standing thigh-deep in a hefty current, and how to get my line out of a tree—over and over again. It was a very educational day overall.

LOWFAT FRUITY GRANOLA

Low
Fat

     2 cups old-fashioned rolled oats
     1 cup puffed millet
   $1/2$ cup toasted wheat germ
   $1/2$ cup honey
   $1/8$ cup molasses
     1 teaspoon vanilla
   $1/2$ teaspoon cinnamon
   $1/2$ teaspoon ginger
   $1/4$ cup applesauce
   $1/2$ cup dried apples, sliced into bits
   $1/4$ cup dried cranberries

   non-stick cooking spray

Preheat the oven to 350°. Spray a large baking sheet with non-stick cooking spray.

Combine the oats, millet, and wheat germ in a large mixing bowl.

In small saucepan, mix the honey, molasses, vanilla, cinnamon, ginger, and applesauce together over medium heat. Stir to combine, but don't bring to a boil. When these ingredients are hot and well blended, pour them over the top of the oat mixture. Stir well to coat the oats with the sweet mixture.

Spread the granola out on the baking sheet. Bake for about 30 minutes, stirring twice, until the granola is golden. Remove from the oven and add the dried fruit while the granola is cooling.

Store in a tightly covered container.

If you use this granola as energy food along the trail (while hiking, biking, etc.), forgo the lowfat substitution of applesauce for butter. Active outdoor enthusiasts need every ounce of fat they can get while on the trail.

Low
Fat

BLACK BEAN AND POTATO
BREAKFAST BURRITOS

1 teaspoon vegetable oil

¼ cup diced onion

1 clove garlic, crushed

½ cup diced green bell pepper

1 4-ounce can green chilies, diced

6 eggs, slightly beaten

½ teaspoon cumin

½ teaspoon oregano

⅛ teaspoon cayenne pepper (or to taste)

1 cup grated Monterey jack cheese

⅔ cup prepared salsa

¾ teaspoon salt

¼ teaspoon black pepper

2 large russet potatoes, baked and cubed with the skins on

2 cups cooked and drained black beans, homemade or canned

10 large flour tortillas

salsa and sour cream for garnish

non-stick cooking spray

Preheat the oven to 375°. Spray a baking sheet with non-stick cooking spray.

In a medium-sized skillet, heat the vegetable oil over medium heat. Cook the onions, garlic, and bell pepper for 5 minutes.

In a large mixing bowl, combine the sautéed vegetables with all the remaining ingredients except the tortillas. Stir to distribute the ingredients well.

Spoon a heaping ½ cup of the filling into a line in the center of each tortilla. Fold the top and bottom in toward the filling, then fold one side flap in and the other over it. Lay the burritos seam side down on the baking sheet.

Spray the tops of the burritos with the cooking spray. Bake for about 20 minutes until crispy and heated through. Serve with salsa and sour cream.

Serves 8–10.

On slow Saturday mornings, my brother-in-law makes giant batches of breakfast burritos, wraps them individually in plastic or foil, and pops them in the freezer—a quick, hearty breakfast for busier Saturday mornings. I've also seen him make a bunch of breakfast burritos, freeze them, and carry them in a cooler for the first morning of his elk camp or for his annual paddle fishing trip on the Missouri River. Of course, you can put anything you want in them, and his always include some type of sausage.

You can freeze the burritos cooked or raw. If wrapped airtight, they will keep well for about three months. It's best to wrap them in plastic and then foil. Just don't forget to pull off the plastic layer, rewrapping the burrito in foil, before you reheat them.

BLUE CORN BISCUITS WITH SAUSAGE-APPLE GRAVY

Biscuits:

1$\frac{1}{3}$ cups unbleached white flour

$\frac{1}{2}$ cup blue cornmeal

$\frac{3}{4}$ teaspoon baking soda

2 teaspoons baking powder

$\frac{1}{2}$ teaspoon salt

$\frac{1}{8}$ teaspoon freshly ground black pepper

$\frac{1}{4}$ teaspoon sage

$\frac{1}{2}$ cup shortening

$\frac{3}{4}$ cup buttermilk

Gravy:

$\frac{3}{4}$ pound of pork sausage

$\frac{1}{4}$ cup diced onion

$\frac{1}{4}$ cup diced celery

3 tablespoons flour

2$\frac{1}{2}$ cups whole milk

$\frac{1}{2}$ teaspoon thyme

$\frac{1}{2}$ teaspoon salt

$\frac{1}{4}$ teaspoon freshly ground black pepper

$\frac{1}{2}$ cup coarsely diced Granny Smith apple

Preheat the oven to 400°.

In a large bowl, combine the flour, cornmeal, baking soda, baking powder, salt, pepper, and sage. Cut the shortening into the flour mixture with a pastry knife (or 2 table knives) until it is pebbly looking. Stir in the buttermilk until a soft dough is formed.

Turn the dough onto a floured surface and knead 6–8 times. Pat the dough to a thickness of $\frac{1}{2}$ inch and cut it into 2$\frac{1}{2}$-inch rounds with a biscuit cutter.

Place the biscuits on an ungreased baking sheet. Bake for about 12 minutes or until lightly browned.

While biscuits are baking, start the gravy: Brown the sausage in a skillet over medium-high heat. Drain the fat from the sausage and add the diced onions and celery. Stir for 3 minutes until the vegetables wilt. Add the flour to the skillet and stir to dissolve well. Slowly add the milk, a little at a time, stirring constantly to prevent lumps. Add the seasonings and stir the gravy until it is bubbly and thickened. Stir in the diced apple and cook until they are just heated through. Serve immediately over hot biscuits.

Serves 6.

For a simple way to make less attractive but equally delicious biscuits, after you have mixed the buttermilk, milk, or beer into your biscuit flour, you don't even have to knead the dough. Leave it lumpy and plop biscuit-sized portions onto the pan. Bake as you normally would.

BAKED OATMEAL CUSTARD WITH DRIED APRICOTS AND ALMONDS

2 cups old-fashioned rolled oats

1½ cups water

3 cups whole milk

4 tablespoons butter

¾ cup diced dried apricots

⅓ cup slivered almonds

1 cup brown sugar

⅛ teaspoon nutmeg

¼ teaspoon ginger

½ teaspoon cinnamon

½ teaspoon salt

4 eggs, slightly beaten

crunchy granola and fresh fruit in season for garnish

non-stick cooking spray

Preheat the oven to 350°. Spray a large casserole dish with non-stick cooking spray.

Place all the ingredients except the eggs in a large saucepan over medium-high heat. Bring to a boil and cook for 2–3 minutes, until the oatmeal starts to plump. Remove from the heat.

Stir ½ cup of the oatmeal mixture into the beaten eggs to temper them. Then whisk the eggs into the rest of the oatmeal. Pour the mixture into the casserole dish. Place casserole dish inside a larger baking pan and pour hot water around the casserole to a depth of 1½ inches. Bake for 35–45 minutes, until the custard is set and not runny in the center. Slice it into squares and serve topped with crunchy granola and fresh fruit.

Serves 4–6.

This recipe, with its mixture of oatmeal and custard ingredients, reminds me of my cooking mentor, Winifred Green Cheney. The author of several best-selling cookbooks for *Southern Living*, Winifred used to invite me over for the grandest lunches I'd ever eaten. She always encouraged me to eat a hearty bowl of old-fashioned hot oatmeal for breakfast so I would stay healthy. She was also known to carry a basket filled with simple baked custards to friends who were feeling less than healthy. Thus, the combination of the two dishes.

Gracious and generous, Winifred has taught me many valued lessons about living and cooking. Her cookbooks always contain a number of recipes created for and dedicated to the Pulitzer Prize-winning Mississippi author Eudora Welty. I don't know of any recipes created just for Winifred, so I've invented this one. With it I honor her gentle and tasty presence in the culinary makeup of her beloved South, as well as the role she played in my own culinary education.

SPICED DUTCH BABY WITH DRIED-APPLE SAUCE

Sauce:

½ cup diced dried apples

1 cup apple juice

1 tablespoon fresh lemon juice

¼ cup chopped walnuts

1 teaspoon cornstarch

4 tablespoons honey

½ teaspoon cinnamon

⅛ teaspoon cloves

2 tablespoons butter

Dutch Baby:

¼ teaspoon ground ginger

½ teaspoon ground cinnamon

¾ cup all-purpose flour

½ teaspoon vanilla

¼ cup butter

3 eggs

¾ cup milk

To prepare the sauce, mix all the sauce ingredients together in a small pan over medium heat. Whisk to combine well and continue stirring until bubbly and thickened. Set aside while making the Dutch Baby.

Preheat the oven to 425°.

To make the Dutch Baby: Stir the spices into the flour and set aside.

Place the butter in a large cast-iron skillet in the preheated oven. While the pan is heating, beat the eggs with an electric mixer for 1 minute on highest speed. Whisk the milk and the flour mixture into the eggs, alternately, until just blended. The batter may still be lumpy.

Pull the skillet out of the oven and pour the batter onto the melted butter. Return the pan to the oven and bake for 20–25 minutes, until brown and puffy.

Slice into wedges at the table and serve immediately with warm dried-apple sauce.

Serves 4.

Dutch Baby may have its own long and colorful camp-cook history, but to me it comes right out of Aunt Fran's kitchen. She still has the tattered, batter-stained, 1970s issue of *Sunset* magazine that her recipe came from. The first time we ever had one, my sister and I were delighted by its magical puffiness as it was pulled out of the hot oven. "You've got to come and see this, girls," Aunt Fran said as she held tight to the heavy cast iron skillet, tipping the pillowy breakfast low enough for us to see. She sprinkled it with powdered sugar and served it with warm maple syrup from a pretty pitcher.

CHOCOLATE-RASPBERRY FRENCH TOAST

4 eggs
1½ cups milk
1 teaspoon vanilla
½ teaspoon cinnamon
12 slices dense white or whole wheat bread
3 tablespoons butter
3 chocolate bars, broken in half
½ cup raspberry jam
powdered sugar

Combine the eggs, milk, vanilla, and cinnamon in a mixing bowl and blend well.

Heat one tablespoon of the butter in a non-stick skillet on medium heat. Dip a slice of bread into the egg mixture and lay it in the heated skillet. Place 1 piece of chocolate on top of the bread and spoon about 3 tablespoons of raspberry jam over the piece of chocolate. Immediately dip a second piece of bread in the egg batter and lay it on top of the jam. Cook until golden on one side, pressing on the top piece of bread with a spatula to help seal the slices together. Carefully flip the stuffed toast over and brown the other side. Remove from the skillet and keep warm in the oven.

Add another tablespoon of butter to the pan for each batch. Two can be prepared in the pan at once.

Slice each toast package in half diagonally on an individual serving plate to allow the chocolate raspberry filling to ooze out. Sprinkle with powdered sugar and serve.

Serves 6.

Decadent, yes. Wrong for breakfast, no. This chocolate-raspberry-stuffed French toast is a way to turn several simple breakfast dishes into an elegant brunch buffet.

Sometimes I only want to prepare one recipe for a meal and fill in with easy, throw-together side dishes. Here's what I would serve with this decadent French toast recipe.

Suggested Menu:

- Mimosas (mix orange juice and champagne to taste)
- Canadian bacon, dipped in maple syrup and browned in a skillet
- Scrambled eggs with basil sprinkled in them
- Fresh strawberries and sliced melon
- Chocolate-Raspberry French Toast

Low
Fat

CHOKECHERRY SYRUP

3 cups water
4 pounds ripe chokecherries
7 cups sugar

Bring the water to a boil in a large, non-reactive stock pot. Add the cherries. Cover and simmer for 20 minutes. Cool well.

Fill a jelly bag with the liquid and cooked fruit and squeeze the juice out into a container.

Add 3$^1/_2$ cups of the juice to the sugar in large pot. Bring the syrup to a boil over medium-high heat, stirring constantly. Lower the heat to medium and keep the syrup at a low boil until the mixture begins to thicken. Remove it from heat.

Skim the foam off with spoon and pour the syrup into jars immediately. Cover the jars with hot paraffin or seal with lids.

Use the leftover juice in more syrup or add to wine vinegar with a bit of sugar for a fruity, tart salad vinegar.

Makes 5–6 pints of syrup.

Chokecherries were one of the main berries Native Americans used to make pemmican. The cherries were dried and cooked into teas and soups as well as mixed with dried meat and lard for the pemmican. Chokecherries were often ground, seeds and all, which seems dangerous in light of the fact that the seeds contain cyanide. Fortunately, when the seeds are heated, the poison is cooked away.

Appendix A
Sources for Rocky Mountain Ingredients

BUFFALO

Denver Buffalo Company
(800) 289-2833 or (303) 831-1299

Rocky Mountain Bison, Inc./High Meadow Buffalo
7320 Country Road 53
Center, CO 81125
(303) 287-7100

Rocky Mountain Natural Meats
6069 Wild Country Road 5
Erie, CO 80516
(303) 287-7100

Wilderness Gourmet
P.O. Box 3257
Ann Arbor, MI 48106
(313) 663-6987

National Buffalo Association
10 Main Street
Fort Pierre, SD 57532
(605) 233-2829
(Call for local sources of buffalo products)

Native Game Company
1105 West Oliver
P.O. Box 1046
Spearfish, SD 57783
(605) 642-2601

GAME BIRDS

Wylie Hill Farm
P.O. Box 35-cc
Craftsbury Common, VT 05827
(802) 586-2887
(quail)

L & L Pheasantry
P.O. Box 298
Hegins, PA 17938
(717) 682-9074
(pheasant, wild turkey, and poussin)

Game Sales International
P.O. Box 5314
Loveland, CO 80538
(303) 667-4090

Native Game Company
1105 West Oliver
P.O. Box 1046
Spearfish, SD 57783
(605) 642-2601
(duck, pheasant, and other game birds)

High Valley Farm, Inc.
14 Alsace Way
Colorado Springs, CO 80906
(719) 634-2944
(pheasant and quail)

Trapper Creek
400 South 147 West
Jerome, ID 83338
(208) 324-7211
(pheasant and quail)

VENISON

Broken Arrow Ranch
104 Junction Highway
Ingram, TX 78025
(800) 962-4263
(fallow and axis venison)

Millbrook Venison Products
RR2, Box 133
Verbank Road
Millbrook, NY 12545
(800) 774-deer or (917) 677-8457

FISH

Mountain Lake Fisheries
P.O. Box 1067
Columbia Falls, MT 59912
(800) 809-0826

Trapper Creek
400 South 147 West
Jerome, ID 83338
(208) 324-7211
(salmon and smoked trout)

Good Taste
P.O. Box 4569
Ketchum, ID 83340
(208) 726-8881

MISCELLANY

My Sante Fe Connection
517 ¹/₂ Central Avenue N.W.
Sante Fe, NM 87102
(505) 842-9564
(green chilies, red chilies, pine nuts, and other
New Mexican products)

Bear Creek Fishery
358 Bear Creek Road
Libby, Montana 59923
(406) 293-6498
(rosehip, huckleberry, and chokecherry jams and
syrups)

Good Taste
P.O. Box 4569
Ketchum, ID 83340
(208) 726-8881
(dried and fresh mushrooms and baking potatoes)

Butterfly Herbs
232 N. Higgins
Missoula, MT
(406) 728-8780
(rosehips, dried herbs, spices, and mushrooms)

Appendix B
One-Hour or Less Recipes

I n d e x

About the Author

A fifth-generation Montanan whose family made their way to the Big Sky state as French Canadian fur trappers, Irish farmers, and Civil War emigrants, Leslie DeDominic is proud to be a Montana native. She was born in Great Falls, Montana, and graduated from high school in Fort Benton, Montana's trading-post birthplace. Having developed a passion for cooking as a summer ranch cook, DeDominic went on to earn a degree in home economics from The University of Montana in Missoula.

DeDominic's path led away from her beloved Rocky Mountains when she moved to College Station, Texas. There, DeDominic began to develop a more culturally diverse style of cooking, creating recipes for Messina Hof Winery, teaching classic Italian, French, and lowfat cooking classes, and serving as the food editor of *Insite*, a Brazos Valley home-living magazine. DeDominic started Helping Hand Home Meals, a dietary analysis and in-home meal service which she owned for two years in Texas and took with her to Jackson, Mississippi. The move to Jackson further broadened the scope of DeDominic's culinary skills as she took advantage of the local cooking school, Everyday Gourmet, and spent two years as the social columnist and feature writer for the *Jackson Clarion Ledger*.

A third move, this time to California, saw DeDominic working as a travel writer in addition to covering local chefs for *Panache* magazine. After six years away, DeDominic made her way back home to Great Falls, where she served as the chef at Paris Gibson Square Museum of Art, was host of a weekly cooking segment on KRTV, and is still the restaurant columnist for the *Great Falls Tribune*. A self-described busybody who is constantly on the move, DeDominic has also taught cooking classes in adult education programs, served as a publicity assistant at the C. M. Russell Museum of Western Art, was manager of the Great Falls Symphony's Cascade Quartet Strings Ensemble, and has been active in a variety of charities, while keeping up a rigorous hiking, fishing, hunting, skiing, and general goofing-off schedule with five-year-old daughter Tessa.

Now a full-time freelance writer and publicist in Fort Benton, Montana, DeDominic can be found cooking for family and friends as she travels around the country with her sidekick Tessa and their faithful dog Gilda.